*A gift for*

..........................................................

*From*

..........................................................

*Date*

...................

# GOD'S PROMISES

*- for the -*

# *Faithful American*

DR. RICHARD LEE & JACK COUNTRYMAN

# CONTENTS

## The Bible and American Presidents

# INTRODUCTION

All people dream of discovering in their lifetime a special secret map that will guide them to hidden treasure. The book you hold in your hand is such a guide. Much of America's rich story is told in these pages, along with many wonderful promises from God's Word that have served as the very foundations upon which our nation was formed.

President Ronald Reagan said, "Within the covers of that single Book are all the answers to all the problems that face us today, if we'd only look there. . . . I hope Americans will read and study the Bible."[1] God's Word and America's story are inseparable.

I hope that as you read, you will enjoy these stories of America's patriots and God's wonderful promises to us all. May God bless you, and may God bless America!

*Dr. Richard G. Lee*

Throughout the history of our country, men and women have looked to God's Word for wisdom, strength, and encouragement. Through His Word, He has guided them as they acknowledged His omnipotence. God's promises come alive when combined with the historical journey of the men and women who formed the foundation of our country. Their dependence on God and His Word has become the brick and mortar for our Christian heritage. Each passage of Scripture has been chosen to help the reader appreciate our history and God's promises.

*Jack Countryman*

# "Thanksgiving Proclamation"

*City of New York, October 3, 1789*

Whereas it is the duty of all Nations to acknowledge the providence of Almighty God, to obey his will, to be grateful for his benefits, and humbly to implore his protection and favor—and whereas both Houses of Congress have by their joint Committee requested me "to recommend to the People of the United States a day of public thanksgiving and prayer to be observed by acknowledging with grateful hearts the many signal favors of Almighty God, especially by affording them an opportunity peaceably to establish a form of government for their safety and happiness."

Now therefore I do recommend and assign Thursday the 26th day of November next to be devoted by the People of these States to the service of that great and glorious Being, who is the beneficent Author of all the good that was, that is, or that will be—That we may then all unite in rendering unto him our sincere and humble thanks—for his kind care and protection of the People of this country previous to their becoming a Nation—for the signal and manifold mercies, and the favorable interpositions of his Providence which we experienced in the course and conclusion of the late war—for the great degree of tranquility, union, and plenty, which we have since enjoyed—for the peaceable and rational manner, in which we have been enabled to establish constitutions of government for our safety and happiness, and particularly the national One now lately instituted—for the civil and religious liberty with which we are blessed; and the means we have of acquiring and diffusing useful knowledge; and in general for all the great and various favors which he hath been pleased to confer upon us.

And also that we may then unite in most humbly offering our prayers and supplications to the great Lord and Ruler of Nations and beseech him to pardon our national and other transgressions—to enable us all, whether in public or private stations, to perform our several and relative duties properly and punctually—to render our national government a blessing to all the People, by constantly being a Government of wise, just and constitutional laws, discreetly and faithfully executed and obeyed—to protect and guide all Sovereigns and Nations (especially such as have shewn kindness unto us) and to bless them with good government, peace, and concord—To promote the knowledge and practice of true religion and virtue, and the encrease of science among them and us—and generally to grant unto all Mankind such a degree of temporal prosperity as he alone knows to be best.[2]

G. Washington

# Praying for Our Nation

FROM OUR NATION'S EARLIEST DAYS, GOD'S PROMISE IN 2 Chronicles 7 that He will hear the cry of a humbled people has motivated America's leaders to call citizens to prayer. In 1775, as it began the process of forming a new nation, the Continental Congress called for a day of prayer. At critical junctures during the Civil War, President Abraham Lincoln called for the nation to fast and pray. And in 1952, President Truman signed a bill establishing an annual National Day of Prayer.

Second Chronicles helps establish a model of national spiritual renewal. The book recounts how a succession of righteous kings in Judah led to reforms that brought the people back to true faith in God. Second Chronicles 16:9 assures us that God will "show Himself strong" toward those who place their trust in Him.

*If My people who are called by My name will humble themselves, and pray and seek My face, and turn from their wicked ways, then I will hear from heaven, and will forgive their sin and heal their land.*

2 CHRONICLES 7:14

*If we confess our sins, He is faithful and just to forgive us our sins and to cleanse us from all unrighteousness.*

1 JOHN 1:9

*Call to Me, and I will answer you, and show you great and mighty things, which you do not know.*

JEREMIAH 33:3

*Save now, I pray, O LORD;*
*O LORD, I pray, send now prosperity.*

PSALM 118:25

# Declaring Independence

ADOPTED ON JULY 4, 1776, THE DECLARATION OF INDEPENDENCE stated that the thirteen American colonies were "Free and Independent States" and that "all political connection between them and the State of Great Britain, is and ought to be totally dissolved."[3] Our Founding Fathers acknowledged God as the source of our rights:

> We hold these truths to be self-evident, that all men are created equal, that they are endowed by their Creator with certain unalienable Rights, that among these are Life, Liberty and the pursuit of Happiness—That to secure these rights, Governments are instituted among Men, deriving their just Powers from the consent of the governed—That whenever any Form of Government becomes destructive of these ends, it is the Right of the People to alter or to abolish it, and to institute new Government, laying its foundation on such principles and organizing its powers in such form, as to them shall seem most likely to effect their Safety and Happiness. . . .
>
> For the support of this Declaration, with a firm reliance on the protection of divine Providence, we mutually pledge to each other our Lives, our Fortunes and our sacred Honor.[4]

*There is therefore now no condemnation to those who are in Christ Jesus, who do not walk according to the flesh, but according to the Spirit. For the law of the Spirit of life in Christ Jesus has made me free from the law of sin and death.*

ROMANS 8:1–2

*Happy is he who has the God of Jacob for his help,*
*Whose hope is in the* LORD *his God,*
*Who made heaven and earth,*
*The sea, and all that is in them;*
*Who keeps truth forever,*
*Who executes justice for the oppressed,*
*Who gives food to the hungry.*
*The* LORD *gives freedom to the prisoners.*

PSALM 146:5–7

*Now the Lord is the Spirit; and where the Spirit of the Lord is, there is liberty.*

2 CORINTHIANS 3:17

# Patriotism Defined

NOAH WEBSTER'S *AN AMERICAN DICTIONARY OF THE ENGLISH Language*, 1828:

> *patriotism,* n. Love of one's country; the passion which aims to serve one's country, either in defending it from invasion, or protecting its rights and maintaining its laws and institutions in vigor and purity. Patriotism is the characteristic of a good citizen, the noblest passion that animates a man in the character of a citizen.[5]

*Merriam-Webster's Collegiate Dictionary, Eleventh Edition*, 2004:

> *patriotism,* n. Love for or devotion to one's country.[6]

Note how the definitions have changed. With its objective actions, Noah Webster's patriotism is very different from the vague, subjective patriotism of one who only feels love for his country. True patriotism is not just an emotional feeling; it is action.

Webster's original definition starts with a love for country but moves to specific actions: service to country, defense of country, protection of the rights of country, maintenance of the laws and institutions of country, and preservation of religion and morality in public and private life.

*And the LORD commanded us to observe all these statutes, to fear the LORD our God, for our good always, that He might preserve us alive, as it is this day.*

DEUTERONOMY 6:24

*Let your heart therefore be loyal to the LORD our God, to walk in His statutes and keep His commandments, as at this day.*

I KINGS 8:61

*So every man of Israel deserted David, and followed Sheba the son of Bichri. But the men of Judah, from the Jordan as far as Jerusalem, remained loyal to their king.*

2 SAMUEL 20:2

*Let every soul be subject to the governing authorities. For there is no authority except from God, and the authorities that exist are appointed by God. . . . Render therefore to all their due: taxes to whom taxes are due . . . fear to whom fear, honor to whom honor.*

ROMANS 13:1, 7

# True History or Consummate Fraud?

HEAR THE CONFIDENT DECLARATION OF AMERICAN STATESman Daniel Webster (1782–1852):

> The Gospel is either true history, or it is a consummate fraud; it is either a reality, or an imposition. Christ was what He professed to be, or He was an imposter. There is no other alternative. His spotless life in His earnest enforcement of the truth, His suffering in its defense, forbid us to suppose that He was following an illusion of a heated brain. Every act of His pure and holy life shows that He was the author of truth, the advocate of truth, the earnest defender of truth, and the uncomplaining sufferer for truth. Now, considering the purity of His doctrines, the simplicity of His life, and the sublimity of His death, is it possible that He would have died for an illusion? In all His preaching the Saviour made no popular appeals. His discourses were all directed to the individual. Christ and His apostles sought to impress upon every man the conviction that he must stand or fall alone—he must live for himself and die for himself, and give up his account to the omniscient God as though he were the only dependent creature in the universe. The Gospel leaves the individual sinner alone with himself and his God.[7]

*For unto us a Child is born,*
*Unto us a Son is given;*
*And the government will be upon His shoulder.*
*And His name will be called*
*Wonderful, Counselor, Mighty God,*
*Everlasting Father, Prince of Peace.*

ISAIAH 9:6

*Now when all things are made subject to Him, then the Son Himself will also be subject to Him who put all things under Him, that God may be all in all.*

I CORINTHIANS 15:28

*Jesus said to him, "I am the way, the truth, and the life. No one comes to the Father except through Me."*

JOHN 14:6

# Investing in Eternity

ELIAS BOUDINOT JR. (1740–1821) WAS AN AMERICAN LAWYER and statesman from Elizabeth, New Jersey. An energetic patriot, he was elected a delegate to the Continental Congress from 1777 to 1784, serving as its president from 1782 to 1783. He then served three terms in Congress and ten years as director of the US Mint. Boudinot supported many civic and educational causes during his life, including serving as one of Princeton's trustees for nearly half a century.

Boudinot was elected president of the American Bible Society at its founding in 1816. In accepting the office, he wrote that this was "the greatest honor" that could have been conferred upon him "this side of the grave."[8] He had an unwavering faith that God had called the men of the society to the work of making Bibles available in America. His ten-thousand-dollar gift, at a time when an annual salary of four hundred dollars was considered good, essentially enabled the formation and organization of the American Bible Society, which still sponsors the work of Bible translation and distribution around the world.

*Therefore gird up the loins of your mind, be sober, and rest your hope fully upon the grace that is to be brought to you at the revelation of Jesus Christ; as obedient children, not conforming yourselves to the former lusts, as in your ignorance; but as He who called you is holy, you also be holy in all your conduct, because it is written, "Be holy, for I am holy."*

I PETER 1:13–16

*Therefore the LORD God of Israel says: "I said indeed that your house and the house of your father would walk before Me forever." But now the LORD says: "Far be it from Me; for those who honor Me I will honor, and those who despise Me shall be lightly esteemed."*

I SAMUEL 2:30

*Do not be deceived, God is not mocked; for whatever a man sows, that he will also reap. For he who sows to his flesh will of the flesh reap corruption, but he who sows to the Spirit will of the Spirit reap everlasting life.*

GALATIANS 6:7–8

# God's Coworker

AGRICULTURAL CHEMIST GEORGE WASHINGTON CARVER (1864–1943) discovered three hundred uses for peanuts and hundreds more uses for soybeans, pecans, and sweet potatoes. Read his thoughts about God:

> As a very small boy exploring the almost virgin woods of the old Carver place, I had the impression someone had just been there ahead of me. Things were so orderly, so clean, so harmoniously beautiful. A few years later in this same woods . . . I was practically overwhelmed with the sense of some Great Presence. Not only had someone been there. Someone was there. . . .
>
> Years later when I read in the Scriptures, "In Him we live and move and have our being," I knew what the writer meant. Never since have I been without this consciousness of the Creator speaking to me. . . . The out-of-doors has been to me more and more a great cathedral in which God could be continuously spoken to and heard from. . . .
>
> Man, who needed a purpose, a mission, to keep him alive, had one. He could be . . . God's co-worker. . . . My purpose alone must be God's purpose—to increase the welfare and happiness of His people. . . . Why, then, should we who believe in Christ be so surprised at what God can do with a willing man in a laboratory?[9]

*Serve the LORD with gladness;*
*Come before His presence with singing.*
*Know that the LORD, He is God;*
*It is He who has made us, and not we ourselves;*
*We are His people and the sheep of His pasture.*

PSALM 100:2–3

*If anyone serves Me, let him follow Me; and where I am, there My servant will be also. If anyone serves Me, him My Father will honor.*

JOHN 12:26

*Let love be without hypocrisy. Abhor what is evil. Cling to what is good. Be kindly affectionate to one another with brotherly love, in honor giving preference to one another; not lagging in diligence, fervent in spirit, serving the Lord; rejoicing in hope, patient in tribulation, continuing steadfastly in prayer; distributing to the needs of the saints, given to hospitality.*

ROMANS 12:9–13

# A Vital Connection

AS FRANKLIN D. ROOSEVELT'S 1939 STATE OF THE UNION underscores, until recent years America's leaders understood the vital connection between religion and democracy. With Hitler on the move in Europe, President Roosevelt said this:

> Storms from abroad directly challenge three institutions indispensable to Americans, now as always. The first is religion. It is the source of the other two—democracy and international good faith.
>
> Religion, by teaching man his relationship to God, gives the individual a sense of his own dignity and teaches him to respect himself by respecting his neighbors.
>
> Democracy, the practice of self-government, is a covenant among free men to respect the rights and liberties of their fellows.
>
> International good faith, a sister of democracy, springs from the will of civilized nations of men to respect the rights and liberties of other nations of men. . . .
>
> There comes a time in the affairs of men when they must prepare to defend, not their homes alone, but the tenets of faith and humanity on which their churches, their governments, and their very civilization are founded. The defense of religion, of democracy, and of good faith among nations is all the same fight. To save one we must now make up our minds to save all.[10]

*For the LORD your God is He who goes with you, to fight for you against your enemies, to save you.*

DEUTERONOMY 20:4

*Watch therefore, and pray always that you may be counted worthy to escape all these things that will come to pass, and to stand before the Son of Man.*

LUKE 21:36

*Therefore be imitators of God as dear children. And walk in love, as Christ also has loved us and given Himself for us, an offering and a sacrifice to God for a sweet-smelling aroma. . . . For you were once darkness, but now you are light in the Lord. Walk as children of light.*

EPHESIANS 5:1–2, 8

*Finally, my brethren, be strong in the Lord and in the power of His might. Put on the whole armor of God, that you may be able to stand against the wiles of the devil.*

EPHESIANS 6:10–11

# Quiet Commitment

LIKE RUTH OF THE OLD TESTAMENT, WOMEN OF STEADFAST loyalty and faith have been key to America's strength. One such woman was Ruth Bell Graham, wife of America's beloved twentieth-century spiritual leader Dr. Billy Graham. Throughout their life together, Dr. Graham often emphasized how vital his wife was to his own success, noting that "my work through the years would have been impossible without her encouragement and support."[11]

For her own part, Mrs. Graham's quiet commitment to her God and to her family reflected the determination of her biblical namesake to follow the God of Israel. Mrs. Graham once explained, "I must faithfully, patiently, lovingly, and happily do my part—then quietly wait for God to do His."[12] That same faithfulness was what led the widowed and desolate Ruth of the Bible to become the wife of Boaz and a member of the line of Jesus Christ.

*All the ways of a man are pure in his own eyes,*
*But the* L*ORD* *weighs the spirits.*
*Commit your works to the* L*ORD*,
*And your thoughts will be established.*

PROVERBS 16:2–3

*Therefore know that the* L*ORD* *your God, He is God, the faithful God who keeps covenant and mercy for a thousand generations with those who love Him and keep His commandments.*

DEUTERONOMY 7:9

*Servants, be submissive to your masters with all fear, not only to the good and gentle, but also to the harsh. For this is commendable, if because of conscience toward God one endures grief, suffering wrongfully.*

I PETER 2:18–19

# Liberty, a Gift from the Creator

FOUNDING FATHER AND ONE OF THE THREE AUTHORS OF *THE Federalist Papers*, Alexander Hamilton (1755–1804), wrote this concerning the nature of liberty:

> The fundamental source of all your errors, sophisms, and false reasonings is a total ignorance of the natural rights of mankind. Were you once to become acquainted with these, you could never entertain a thought that all men are not, by nature, entitled to a parity of privileges. You would be convinced, that natural liberty is a gift of the beneficent Creator to the whole human race, and that civil liberty is founded in that; and cannot be wrested from any people, without the most manifest violation of justice.[13]

*And because you are sons, God has sent forth the Spirit of His Son into your hearts, crying out, "Abba, Father!" Therefore you are no longer a slave but a son, and if a son, then an heir of God through Christ.*

GALATIANS 4:6–7

*The Spirit of the LORD is upon Me,*
*Because He has anointed Me*
*To preach the gospel to the poor;*
*He has sent Me to heal the brokenhearted,*
*To proclaim liberty to the captives*
*And recovery of sight to the blind,*
*To set at liberty those who are oppressed.*

LUKE 4:18

*For you, brethren, have been called to liberty; only do not use liberty as an opportunity for the flesh, but through love serve one another. For all the law is fulfilled in one word, even in this: "You shall love your neighbor as yourself."*

GALATIANS 5:13–14

# "To Live Is Christ"

THE APOSTLE PAUL'S LETTER TO BELIEVERS IN PHILIPPI IS A NOTE of thanks for their help during his time of need. He also lovingly urged the members of the church there to center their actions and thoughts on the pursuit of the person and power of Christ. Paul's central point was simple: Only in Christ are real unity and genuine joy possible. With Christ as our model of humility and service, we believers can enjoy a oneness of purpose, attitude, goal, and labor. Paul then reminded the Philippians that their ultimate citizenship is in heaven.

However, the words of Adlai Stevenson (1900–1965), who served as the US ambassador to the United Nations from 1961 to 1965, remind us of the privilege of being an American citizen:

> When an American says he loves his country, he means not only that he loves the New England hills, the prairies glistening in the sun, or the wide rising plains, the mountains and the seas. He means that he loves an inner air, an inner light in which freedom lives and in which a man can draw the breath of self-respect.[14]

*Yet indeed I also count all things loss for the excellence of the knowledge of Christ Jesus my Lord, for whom I have suffered the loss of all things, and count them as rubbish, that I may gain Christ and be found in Him, not having my own righteousness, which is from the law, but that which is through faith in Christ, the righteousness which is from God by faith; that I may know Him and the power of His resurrection, and the fellowship of His sufferings, being conformed to His death.*

PHILIPPIANS 3:8–10

*Brethren, I do not count myself to have apprehended; but one thing I do, forgetting those things which are behind and reaching forward to those things which are ahead, I press toward the goal for the prize of the upward call of God in Christ Jesus.*

PHILIPPIANS 3:13–14

*For the LORD God is a sun and shield;*
*The LORD will give grace and glory;*
*No good thing will He withhold*
*From those who walk uprightly.*

PSALM 84:11

# Speak Up!

AS A YOUNG PASTOR, TITUS FACED THE DIFFICULT ASSIGNMENT of setting in order the church at Crete. Paul advised him to appoint elders, men of proven spiritual character in their homes and businesses, to do the work of the church. In addition, Paul discussed in his letter to Titus that men and women, young and old, all have vital functions to fulfill in the church if they are to be living examples of the doctrine they profess.

Consider the wisdom of this statement attributed to Dr. Martin Luther King Jr., the great civil rights leader of the twentieth century: "Our lives begin to end the day we become silent about things that matter." If King did not say it, he certainly lived it. Likewise, Paul told Titus that he could not be silent about the greatest matter in human history: "The grace of God that brings salvation has appeared to all men" (Titus 2:11). Paul charged Titus to "speak these things, exhort, and rebuke with all authority" (v. 15).

*But as for you, speak the things which are proper for sound doctrine: that the older men be sober, reverent, temperate, sound in faith, in love, in patience; the older women likewise, that they be reverent in behavior, not slanderers, not given to much wine, teachers of good things—that they admonish the young women to love their husbands, to love their children, to be discreet, chaste, homemakers, good, obedient to their own husbands, that the word of God may not be blasphemed. Likewise, exhort the young men to be sober-minded, in all things showing yourself to be a pattern of good works; in doctrine showing integrity, reverence, incorruptibility.*

TITUS 2:1–7

*Let no one despise your youth, but be an example to the believers in word, in conduct, in love, in spirit, in faith, in purity. Till I come, give attention to reading, to exhortation, to doctrine. Do not neglect the gift that is in you, which was given to you by prophecy with the laying on of the hands of the eldership. Meditate on these things; give yourself entirely to them, that your progress may be evident to all.*

I TIMOTHY 4:12–15

# A More Just Society

THE CIVIL RIGHTS MOVEMENT OF THE 1950S AND 1960S WAS LED primarily by Dr. Martin Luther King Jr., who had become pastor of Dexter Avenue Baptist Church in Montgomery, Alabama, in 1954. At that time, American society was characterized by inequality, oppression, and segregation of Black citizens, fueled by hatred, prejudice, and hostility. Refusing to stoop to such hatred and succumb to any bitterness, Dr. King connected his deep love for God and for his fellow man with the powerful determination to gain equal civil rights for Black people in America.

Dr. King rose to national prominence as the leader of the movement through nonviolent mass demonstrations. The first was the Montgomery, Alabama, bus boycott in 1956, which started after Rosa Parks was arrested for refusing to give her seat on a bus to a white man. The movement produced scores of men and women who risked, and some who gave, their lives to secure a more just and inclusive society.

*Now the Lord is the Spirit; and where the Spirit of the Lord is, there is liberty.*

2 CORINTHIANS 3:17

*"And you shall love the* L*ORD your God with all your heart, with all your soul, with all your mind, and with all your strength." This is the first commandment. And the second, like it, is this: "You shall love your neighbor as yourself." There is no other commandment greater than these.*

MARK 12:30–31

*He who is faithful in what is least is faithful also in much; and he who is unjust in what is least is unjust also in much. Therefore if you have not been faithful in the unrighteous mammon, who will commit to your trust the true riches? And if you have not been faithful in what is another man's, who will give you what is your own? "No servant can serve two masters; for either he will hate the one and love the other, or else he will be loyal to the one and despise the other. You cannot serve God and mammon."*

LUKE 16:10–13

# The Godly Use of Power

IN HIS JANUARY 20, 1989, INAUGURAL ADDRESS, GEORGE H. W. Bush said this:

> We meet on democracy's front porch, a good place to talk as neighbors and as friends. For this is a day when our nation is made whole, when our differences, for a moment, are suspended.
>
> And my first act as President is a prayer. I ask you to bow your heads:
>
> Heavenly Father, we bow our heads and thank You for Your love. Accept our thanks for the peace that yields this day and the shared faith that makes its continuance likely. Make us strong to do Your work, willing to heed and hear Your will, and write on our hearts these words: "Use power to help people." For we are given power not to advance our own purposes, nor to make a great show in the world, nor a name. There is but one just use of power, and it is to serve people. Help us to remember it, Lord. Amen.[15]

*Yet it shall not be so among you; but whoever desires to become great among you shall be your servant.*

MARK 10:43

*And the King will answer and say to them, "Assuredly, I say to you, inasmuch as you did it to one of the least of these My brethren, you did it to Me."*

MATTHEW 25:40

*And He sat down, called the twelve, and said to them, "If anyone desires to be first, he shall be last of all and servant of all."*

MARK 9:35

*He who loves his life will lose it, and he who hates his life in this world will keep it for eternal life. If anyone serves Me, let him follow Me; and where I am, there My servant will be also. If anyone serves Me, him My Father will honor.*

JOHN 12:25–26

# "Sail On, O Ship of State!"

HENRY WADSWORTH LONGFELLOW (1807–1882) WAS ONE OF the most widely known American poets in his day. Reflecting his fervent abolitionist convictions, "The Building of the Ship" speaks of his fear that the slavery issue would destroy the nation.

Thou, too, sail on, O Ship of State!
Sail on, O Union, strong and great!
Humanity with all its fears,
With all the hopes of future years,
Is hanging breathless on thy fate! . . .
Our hearts, our hopes, are all with thee,
Our hearts, our hopes, our prayers, our tears,
Our faith triumphant o'er our fears,
Are all with thee,—are all with thee![16]

In January 1941, President Franklin D. Roosevelt included the first five lines of Longfellow's poem in a handwritten letter to the prime minister of the United Kingdom, Winston Churchill, and said the verse "applies to you people as it does to us."[17] Deeply moved, Churchill saw the letter as a symbol of the two countries' growing partnership. "Give us the tools," he told the president, "and we will finish the job!"[18]

*The LORD brings the counsel of the nations to nothing;*
*He makes the plans of the peoples of no effect.*
*The counsel of the LORD stands forever,*
*The plans of His heart to all generations.*
*Blessed is the nation whose God is the LORD,*
*The people He has chosen as His own inheritance.*

PSALM 33:10–12

*For to this end I also wrote, that I might put you to the test, whether you are obedient in all things. Now whom you forgive anything, I also forgive. For if indeed I have forgiven anything, I have forgiven that one for your sakes in the presence of Christ.*

2 CORINTHIANS 2:9–10

*There is no wisdom or understanding*
*Or counsel against the LORD.*
*The horse is prepared for the day of battle,*
*But deliverance is of the LORD.*

PROVERBS 21:30–31

# "The Last Best Hope of Man"

ON JANUARY 25, 1974, RONALD REAGAN GAVE HIS FAMOUS "Shining City Upon a Hill" speech and concluded by saying this:

> We cannot escape our destiny, nor should we try to. The leadership of the free world was thrust upon us two centuries ago in that little hall in Philadelphia. In the days following World War II, when the economic strength and power of America was all that stood between the world and the return to the dark ages, Pope Pius XII said, "The American people have a great genius for splendid and unselfish actions. Into the hands of America, God has placed the destinies of an afflicted mankind."[19]

We were indeed—and we are today—the last best hope of man on earth.

*Through whom also we have access by faith into this grace in which we stand, and rejoice in hope of the glory of God. . . . Now hope does not disappoint, because the love of God has been poured out in our hearts by the Holy Spirit who was given to us.*

ROMANS 5:2, 5

*For we were saved in this hope, but hope that is seen is not hope; for why does one still hope for what he sees? But if we hope for what we do not see, we eagerly wait for it with perseverance.*

ROMANS 8:24–25

*There is one body and one Spirit, just as you were called in one hope of your calling; one Lord, one faith, one baptism; one God and Father of all, who is above all, and through all, and in you all.*

EPHESIANS 4:4–6

# A Reawakening

PRESIDENT HARRY S. TRUMAN HELD OFFICE DURING THE END of World War II. In this 1946 speech, he reminded Americans of what we fought for and how to preserve it:

> We have just come through a decade in which forces of evil in various parts of the world have been lined up in a bitter fight to banish from the face of the earth . . . religion and democracy. For these forces of evil have long realized that both religion and democracy are founded on one basic principle, the worth and dignity of the individual man and woman. Dictatorship, on the other hand, has always rejected that principle. Dictatorship, by whatever name, is founded on the doctrine that the individual amounts to nothing; that the State is the only thing that counts; and that men and women and children were put on earth solely for the purpose of serving the State. . . .
>
> If men and nations would but live by the precepts of the ancient prophets and the teachings of the Sermon on the Mount, problems which now seem so difficult would soon disappear. . . .
>
> This is a supreme opportunity for the Church to continue to fulfill its mission on earth. . . . Oh for an Isaiah or a Saint Paul to reawaken this sick world to its moral responsibilities![20]

*But seek first the kingdom of God and His righteousness, and all these things shall be added to you.*

MATTHEW 6:33

*The way of the just is uprightness;*
*O Most Upright,*
*You weigh the path of the just.*
*Yes, in the way of Your judgments,*
*O LORD, we have waited for You;*
*The desire of our soul is for Your name*
*And for the remembrance of You.*

ISAIAH 26:7–8

*Delight yourself also in the LORD,*
*And He shall give you the desires of your heart.*
*Commit your way to the LORD,*
*Trust also in Him,*
*And He shall bring it to pass.*
*He shall bring forth your righteousness as the light,*
*And your justice as the noonday.*

PSALM 37:4–6

# Acknowledging God

WHILE THERE HAVE BEEN REVISIONS TO STATE CONSTITUTIONS over the years, forty-three states acknowledge God or a higher power in their preambles, and the other seven states acknowledge God in their religious freedom provisions.

The following are short samples from some of these state constitutions:

> **Connecticut's 1818 Preamble:** "The People of Connecticut, acknowledging with gratitude the good Providence of God in having permitted them to enjoy a free government. . . ."[21]
>
> **Maine's 1820 Preamble:** "We the People of Maine . . . acknowledging with grateful hearts the goodness of the Sovereign Ruler of the Universe in affording us an opportunity . . . and, imploring His aid and direction in its accomplishment. . . ."[22]
>
> **Massachusetts's 1780 Preamble:** "We, therefore, the people of Massachusetts, acknowledging, with grateful hearts, the goodness of the great Legislator of the universe, in affording us, in the course of His providence, an opportunity . . . and devoutly imploring His direction. . . ."[23]

*But let all those rejoice who put their trust in You;*
*Let them ever shout for joy, because You defend them;*
*Let those also who love Your name*
*Be joyful in You.*
*For You, O LORD, will bless the righteous;*
*With favor You will surround him as with a shield.*

PSALM 5:11–12

*The LORD knows the days of the upright,*
*And their inheritance shall be forever.*
*They shall not be ashamed in the evil time,*
*And in the days of famine they shall be satisfied.*

PSALM 37:18–19

*The LORD is righteous in all His ways,*
*Gracious in all His works.*
*The LORD is near to all who call upon Him,*
*To all who call upon Him in truth.*

PSALM 145:17–18

# Faithful to the End

SHORTLY BEFORE 1:00 A.M. ON FEBRUARY 2, 1943, THE AMERICAN transport ship *Dorchester* was steaming through the icy North Atlantic from Newfoundland toward an American base in Greenland, carrying 902 servicemen, merchant seamen, and civilian workers, when a German torpedo struck the starboard side.

Through the pandemonium, four US Army chaplains—George L. Fox, Methodist; Alexander D. Goode, Jewish; John P. Washington, Roman Catholic; and Clark V. Poling, Dutch Reformed—brought hope to the men struggling to survive, even taking off their own life vests and giving them to four frightened young men.

Then in the darkness, singing and shouting biblical encouragement, the four chaplains linked arms and grasped the railing of the ship as it slipped into the ocean. William Bednar said that as he floated among dead comrades, "their voices were the only thing that kept me going."[24]

Of the men aboard the *Dorchester*, 672 died, including the chaplains. Their heroic conduct offered a vision of greatness that stunned America.

*Greater love has no one than this, than to lay down one's life for his friends.*

JOHN 15:13

*My covenant I will not break,*
*Nor alter the word that has gone out of My lips.*
*Once I have sworn by My holiness;*
*I will not lie to David:*
*His seed shall endure forever,*
*And his throne as the sun before Me;*
*It shall be established forever like the moon,*
*Even like the faithful witness in the sky.*

PSALM 89:34–37

*I am the good shepherd. The good shepherd gives His life for the sheep.*

JOHN 10:11

# The Bible and American Presidents

*The first, and almost the only book, deserving such universal recommendation, is the Bible. . . . I speak as a man of the world, and I say to you, "Search the Scriptures!"*

John Quincy Adams, 6th president[25]

*In regard for this Great Book, I have but to say, it is the best gift God has given to man. All the good the Savior gave to the world was communicated through this book.*

Abraham Lincoln, 16th president[26]

*We cannot read the history of our rise and development as a Nation, without reckoning with the place the Bible has occupied in shaping the advances of the Republic. . . . Where we have been the truest and most consistent in obeying its precepts, we have attained the greatest measure of contentment and prosperity.*

Franklin D. Roosevelt, 32nd president[27]

*The foundations of our society and our Government rest so much on the teachings of the Bible that it would be difficult to support them if faith in these teachings would cease to be practically universal in our country.*

Calvin Coolidge, 30th president[28]

*If you blot out of your statute, book, your Constitution, your family life, all that is taken from the Sacred Book, what would there be left to bind society together?*

BENJAMIN HARRISON, 23RD PRESIDENT[29]

*Within the covers of that single Book are all the answers to all the problems that face us today. . . . The Bible can touch our hearts, order our minds, refresh our souls.*

RONALD REAGAN, 40TH PRESIDENT[30]

*The fundamental basis of this Nation's law was given to Moses on the Mount. The fundamental basis of our Bill of Rights comes from the teachings we get from Exodus and Saint Matthew, from Isaiah and Saint Paul. . . . If we don't have a proper fundamental moral background, we will finally end up with a totalitarian government which does not believe in rights for anybody except the state.*

HARRY S. TRUMAN, 33RD PRESIDENT[31]

# "Duty to God"

THE BOY SCOUTS OF AMERICA (NOW CALLED SCOUTING America) believes that no member can grow into the best kind of citizen without recognizing an obligation to God. Accordingly, members and leaders obligate themselves to do their duty to God and live in accordance with the Scout Oath and the Scout Law. But it hasn't been without its share of legal battles.

In *Welsh v. Boy Scouts of America* (1993), the US Court of Appeals for the Seventh Circuit ruled that the Boy Scouts could keep the phrase *duty to God* in their oath and that, as a private organization, they have the right to exclude anyone who refuses to take the oath:

> The leadership of many in our government is a testimonial to the success of Boy Scout activities. In recent years, single-parent families, gang activity, availability of drugs and other factors have increased the dire need for support structures like the Scouts. When the government, in this instance through the courts, seeks to regulate the membership of an organization like the Boy Scouts in a way that scuttles its founding principles, we run the risk of undermining one of the seedbeds of virtue that cultivate the sorts of citizens our nation so desperately needs.[32]

Cases in 1995 and 1998 also upheld the "duty to God" requirements.

*So you shall serve the Lord your God, and He will bless your bread and your water. And I will take sickness away from the midst of you.*

EXODUS 23:25

*The Lord our God we will serve, and His voice we will obey!*

JOSHUA 24:24

*And now, Israel, what does the Lord your God require of you, but to fear the Lord your God, to walk in all His ways and to love Him, to serve the Lord your God with all your heart and with all your soul.*

DEUTERONOMY 10:12

# Answers from the Bible

JOHN MCLEAN (1785–1861), A US POSTMASTER GENERAL AND justice of the US Supreme Court, wrote this:

> No one can estimate or describe the salutary influences of the Bible. What would the world be without it? Compare the dark places of the earth, where the light of the gospel has not penetrated, with those where it has been proclaimed and embraced in all its purity. Life and immortality are brought to light by the Scriptures. Aside from Revelation, darkness rests upon this world, and upon the future. There is no ray of light to shine upon our pathway; there is no star of hope. We begin our speculations as to our destiny in conjecture, and they end in uncertainty. We know not that there is a God, a heaven, or a hell, or any day of general account, when the wicked and the righteous shall be judged. The Bible has shed a glorious light upon our world. It shows us that in the coming day we must answer for the deeds done in the body. It has opened us to a new and living way, so plainly marked that no one can mistake it.[33]

*For it is the God who commanded light to shine out of darkness, who has shone in our hearts to give the light of the knowledge of the glory of God in the face of Jesus Christ.*

2 CORINTHIANS 4:6

*For the word of God is living and powerful, and sharper than any two-edged sword, piercing even to the division of soul and spirit, and of joints and marrow, and is a discerner of the thoughts and intents of the heart.*

HEBREWS 4:12

*Every word of God is pure;*
*He is a shield to those who put their trust in Him.*

PROVERBS 30:5

*So then faith comes by hearing, and hearing by the word of God.*

ROMANS 10:17

# "Ask Not"

WITH AMERICANS FEARING WAR, PRESIDENT JOHN F. KENNEDY spoke these inspirational words in his 1961 inaugural address:

> The torch has been passed to a new generation of American—born in this century, tempered by war, disciplined by a hard and bitter peace, proud of our ancient heritage—and unwilling to witness or permit the slow undoing of those human rights to which this nation has always been committed. . . .
>
> In the long history of the world, only a few generations have been granted the role of defending freedom in its hour of maximum danger. . . . The energy, the faith, the devotion which we bring to this endeavor will light our country and all who serve it—and the glow from that fire can truly light the world. And so, my fellow Americans: ask not what your country can do for you—ask what you can do for your country. . . .
>
> With a good conscience our only sure reward, with history the final judge of our deeds, let us go forth to lead the land we love, asking His blessing and His help, but knowing that here on earth God's work must truly be our own.[34]

*But as for me and my house, we will serve the* L*ORD.*

JOSHUA 24:15

*Delight yourself also in the* L*ORD,*
*And He shall give you the desires of your heart.*

PSALM 37:4

*And you will seek Me and find Me, when you search for Me with all your heart.*

JEREMIAH 29:13

*Then [Ananias] said, "The God of our fathers has chosen you that you should know His will, and see the Just One, and hear the voice of His mouth."*

ACTS 22:14

# Christ Reigns Supreme

IN THE EARLY CHURCH, MANY BELIEVERS WHO HAD STEPPED out of Judaism into Christianity found themselves persecuted by nonbelieving Jews, prompting the writer of Hebrews to address the superiority of Christ over Judaism. Christ is superior to angels, the Aaronic priesthood, and the law. In short, he argued, there is infinitely more to be gained by following Christ than to be lost by yielding up the Jewish traditions.

The recipients of the book of Hebrews faced persecution, even death, for their Christian confession, and it is worth noting that the marching song of the Union Army during the Civil War included the line "as He died to make men holy, let us die to make men free."[35] Although that phrase was later changed to "let us live to make men free,"[36] for the soldiers who placed their lives on the line to end slavery and preserve the Union, the original wording was absolutely correct.

*Seeing then that we have a great High Priest who has passed through the heavens, Jesus the Son of God, let us hold fast our confession.*

HEBREWS 4:14

*Likewise the Spirit also helps in our weaknesses. For we do not know what we should pray for as we ought, but the Spirit Himself makes intercession for us with groanings which cannot be uttered. Now He who searches the hearts knows what the mind of the Spirit is, because He makes intercession for the saints according to the will of God.*

ROMANS 8:26–27

*Therefore He is also able to save to the uttermost those who come to God through Him, since He always lives to make intercession for them. For such a High Priest was fitting for us, who is holy, harmless, undefiled, separate from sinners, and has become higher than the heavens.*

HEBREWS 7:25–26

# The Goal of Government

WHEN THE FIRST SETTLERS ARRIVED IN AMERICA, THE INFLUence of the Bible on their lives came with them. For many, their Christian faith was as much a part of who they were as their brave spirit was, and their faith impacted everything they did. This fact stands out boldly as one sees, again and again, Scripture reflected in the individual colonies' statements of the goal of their government. An early Rhode Island charter from 1638, for instance, begins this way: "We . . . submit our persons, lives and estates unto our Lord Jesus Christ, the King of kings and Lord of lords, and to all those perfect and most absolute laws of his given us in his holy word."[37]

In fact, from the first colony at Jamestown to the Pennsylvania Charter of Privileges granted to William Penn in 1701—where "all Persons who . . . profess to believe in Jesus Christ, the Saviour of the World, shall be capable . . . to serve this Government in any capacity, both legislatively and executively"[38]—the Bible was considered the rule of life in the colonies.

*The counsel of the* LORD *stands forever,*
*The plans of His heart to all generations.*
*Blessed is the nation whose God is the* LORD*,*
*The people He has chosen as His own inheritance.*

PSALM 33:11–12

*But the Helper, the Holy Spirit, whom the Father will send in My name, He will teach you all things, and bring to your remembrance all things that I said to you.*

JOHN 14:26

*They have forsaken the right way and gone astray, following the way of Balaam the son of Beor, who loved the wages of unrighteousness; but he was rebuked for his iniquity: a dumb donkey speaking with a man's voice restrained the madness of the prophet.*

*These are wells without water, clouds carried by a tempest, for whom is reserved the blackness of darkness forever.*

2 PETER 2:15–17

# Abraham Lincoln on Skepticism

A CLOSE FRIEND OF ABE LINCOLN, JOSHUA SPEED, PUBLISHED *Reminiscences of Abraham Lincoln*, which includes a story from 1864 when he visited Lincoln:

> When I knew [Mr. Lincoln], in early life, he was a skeptic. He had tried hard to be a believer, but his reason could not grasp and solve the great problem of redemption as taught. . . . But this was a subject we never discussed.
>
> The only evidence I have of any change, was in the summer before he was killed. I was invited out to the Soldier's Home to spend the night. As I entered the room, near night, he was sitting near a window intently reading his Bible.
>
> Approaching him I said, "I am glad to see you so profitably engaged."
>
> "Yes," said he, "I am profitably engaged."
>
> "Well," said I, "if you have recovered from your skepticism, I am sorry to say that I have not."
>
> Looking me earnestly in the face and placing his hand on my shoulder, he said, "You are wrong, Speed. Take all of this book upon reason that you can, and the balance on faith, and you will live and die a happier and better man."[39]

*Thomas, because you have seen Me, you have believed. Blessed are those who have not seen and yet have believed.*

JOHN 20:29

*If any of you lacks wisdom, let him ask of God, who gives to all liberally and without reproach, and it will be given to him. But let him ask in faith, with no doubting, for he who doubts is like a wave of the sea driven and tossed by the wind.*

JAMES 1:5–6

*Have faith in God. For assuredly, I say to you, whoever says to this mountain, "Be removed and be cast into the sea," and does not doubt in his heart, but believes that those things he says will be done, he will have whatever he says.*

MARK 11:22–23

# Finding Hope in Suffering

THE APOSTLE PETER WROTE THE WORDS WE FIND IN 1 PETER to persecuted believers, encouraging them to persevere for the person and message of Christ. Peter provided them with a divine perspective on their trials so they could endure them without wavering in their faith. Having been born again to a living hope, they were to imitate the Holy One who Himself suffered and to rely on His strong presence when they suffer.

As commander of the Allied forces in Europe during World War II and later president of the United States, Dwight D. Eisenhower also knew a great deal about the strength of men and women in difficult times. He said in remembrance of D-Day, "The spirit of man is more important than mere physical strength, and the spiritual fiber of a nation than its wealth."[40] In a letter to the American Bible Society, he wrote, "The Bible is endorsed by the ages. Our civilization is built upon its words. In no other book is there such a collection of inspired wisdom, reality, and hope."[41]

*Beloved, do not think it strange concerning the fiery trial which is to try you, as though some strange thing happened to you; but rejoice to the extent that you partake of Christ's sufferings, that when His glory is revealed, you may also be glad with exceeding joy.*

I PETER 4:12–13

*And if children, then heirs—heirs of God and joint heirs with Christ, if indeed we suffer with Him, that we may also be glorified together. For I consider that the sufferings of this present time are not worthy to be compared with the glory which shall be revealed in us.*

ROMANS 8:17–18

*My brethren, count it all joy when you fall into various trials, knowing that the testing of your faith produces patience. But let patience have its perfect work, that you may be perfect and complete, lacking nothing.*

JAMES 1:2–4

# Entertaining Strangers

NICKNAMED "THE GRAND CENTRAL STATION OF THE Underground Railroad," the home of Levi and Catharine Coffin in Cincinnati—just across the Ohio River from Kentucky—became a natural stopover for enslaved people escaping from the South to the free state of Ohio.[42]

When the Fugitive Slave Act was passed in 1850, making it illegal to aid a runaway enslaved person under threat of imprisonment or a fine, Catharine and Levi made no change in their activities. To their critics, they invariably replied that according to Scripture, they were dutybound to help any individual who came to their door.[43]

While some might have grown weary of the constant stream of visitors, Catharine cheerfully served the refugees by cooking for them, collecting donations, washing their clothing, listening to their troubles, helping them find employment, and assisting in smuggling them to safer locations.

In her warm and hospitable home, she offered to many their first experience of interracial friendship and Christian care.

*Be kindly affectionate to one another with brotherly love, in honor giving preference to one another; not lagging in diligence, fervent in spirit, serving the Lord; rejoicing in hope, patient in tribulation, continuing steadfastly in prayer; distributing to the needs of the saints, given to hospitality.*

ROMANS 12:10–13

*Therefore, as we have opportunity, let us do good to all, especially to those who are of the household of faith.*

GALATIANS 6:10

*If there is among you a poor man of your brethren . . . you shall not harden your heart nor shut your hand from your poor brother, but you shall open your hand wide to him and willingly lend him sufficient for his need, whatever he needs.*

DEUTERONOMY 15:7–8

# "A Christian Nation"

IN THE 1892 CASE *THE CHURCH OF THE HOLY TRINITY V. UNITED States*, the US Supreme Court determined that an English minister was not a foreign laborer. The court considered America's Christian identity to be a strong support for concluding that Congress could not have intended to prohibit foreign ministers.

Justice David Josiah Brewer stated that the US was a "Christian nation."[44] The court had already demonstrated the country's religious character with eighty-seven examples from pre-Constitutional documents, historical practice, and colonial charters, that reveal religious roots.

> This is a religious people. . . . From the discovery of this continent to the present hour, there is a single voice making this affirmation. . . . There is no dissonance in these declarations. There is a universal language pervading them all, having one meaning; they affirm and reaffirm that this is a religious nation. These are not individual sayings. . . . They speak the voice of the entire people.[45]

Brewer later clarified his position: Many American traditions are rooted in Christianity, but Christianity should not receive legal privileges or be established to the exclusion of other religions or irreligion.

*But you are a chosen generation, a royal priesthood, a holy nation, His own special people, that you may proclaim the praises of Him who called you out of darkness into His marvelous light.*

I PETER 2:9

*Then it shall come to pass, because you listen to these judgments, and keep and do them, that the* LORD *your God will keep with you the covenant and the mercy which He swore to your fathers.*

DEUTERONOMY 7:12

*And the Scripture, foreseeing that God would justify the Gentiles by faith, preached the gospel to Abraham beforehand, saying, "In you all the nations shall be blessed." So then those who are of faith are blessed with believing Abraham.*

GALATIANS 3:8–9

# The Faith of the Founders

MUCH HAS BEEN WRITTEN IN RECENT YEARS TO TRY TO DISMISS the fact that America was founded upon the biblical principles of Judeo-Christianity, but all the revisionism in the world cannot change the facts. Anyone who examines the original writings, personal correspondence, biographies, and public statements of the individuals who were instrumental in the founding of America will find an abundance of quotations showing the profound extent to which their thinking and their lives were influenced by a Christian worldview.

That is not to say that all of the Founding Fathers were Christians. Such is not the case, but even those who were not Christians were deeply influenced by the principles of Christianity. We can easily get so distracted, wondering whether Benjamin Franklin or Thomas Jefferson ever put their personal faith in Jesus Christ, that we can miss the important fact that almost all the Founders thought from a biblical perspective, whether or not they believed.

*Because of your unbelief; for assuredly, I say to you, if you have faith as a mustard seed, you will say to this mountain, "Move from here to there," and it will move; and nothing will be impossible for you.*

MATTHEW 17:20

*Therefore, having been justified by faith, we have peace with God through our Lord Jesus Christ, through whom also we have access by faith into this grace in which we stand, and rejoice in hope of the glory of God.*

ROMANS 5:1–2

*And let us not grow weary while doing good, for in due season we shall reap if we do not lose heart.*

GALATIANS 6:9

*Now faith is the substance of things hoped for, the evidence of things not seen.*

HEBREWS 11:1

# Protecting the Foundations

JEDIDIAH MORSE (1761–1826) WAS A PIONEER AMERICAN EDUCAtor, clergyman, geographer, and father of Samuel Morse, inventor of the telegraph and Morse code. Jedidiah studied for the ministry at Yale and, in 1789, accepted a call to the First Church of Charlestown, Massachusetts. He was alarmed by how far the clergy had moved from doctrinal orthodoxy. In a 1799 sermon, he said the following:

> Our dangers are of two kinds, those which affect our religion, and those which affect our government. They are, however, so closely allied that they cannot, with propriety, be separated. . . .
>
> To the kindly influence of Christianity we owe that degree of civil freedom, and political and social happiness . . . mankind now enjoy. In proportion as the genuine effects of Christianity are diminished in any nation . . . in the same proportion will the people of that nation recede from the blessings of genuine freedom. . . . It follows, that all efforts made to destroy the foundations of our holy religion, ultimately tend to the subversion also of our political freedom and happiness. Whenever the pillars of Christianity shall be overthrown, our present republican forms of government, and all the blessings which flow from them, must fall with them.[46]

*According to the grace of God which was given to me, as a wise master builder I have laid the foundation, and another builds on it. But let each one take heed how he builds on it. For no other foundation can anyone lay than that which is laid, which is Jesus Christ.*

I CORINTHIANS 3:10–11

*Nevertheless the solid foundation of God stands, having this seal: "The Lord knows those who are His," and, "Let everyone who names the name of Christ depart from iniquity."*

2 TIMOTHY 2:19

*In the LORD I put my trust;*
*How can you say to my soul,*
*"Flee as a bird to your mountain"? . . .*
*If the foundations are destroyed,*
*What can the righteous do?*

PSALM 11:1, 3

# An American Hero

BETWEEN 1957 AND 1975, A HEATED PART OF THE COLD WAR between the Soviet Union and the United States was competition in the realm of space exploration because of its potential military and technological applications, as well as its morale-boosting social benefits. The Soviets took the lead in the Space Race when they were the first to achieve a manned orbit of the earth in 1961. But on February 20, 1962, atop an Atlas rocket, Colonel John Glenn piloted the first American manned orbital mission aboard *Friendship 7*, circling the globe three times. Taking this step toward fulfilling America's political and scientific hopes and dreams, Glenn returned to Earth as virtually every American's hero.

In 1998, NASA invited John Glenn to join the space shuttle *Discovery* crew. On October 29, 1998, he became the oldest human, at the age of seventy-seven, to venture into space. As Glenn observed the heavens and Earth from the windows of *Discovery*, he said, "To look out at this kind of creation out here and not believe in God is to me impossible. It just strengthens my faith. I wish there were words to describe what it's like."[47]

*The heavens declare the glory of God;*
*And the firmament shows His handiwork.*

PSALM 19:1

*Let the heavens declare His righteousness,*
*For God Himself is Judge.*

PSALM 50:6

*The heavens are Yours, the earth also is Yours;*
*The world and all its fullness, You have*
*founded them.*

PSALM 89:11

*Before the mountains were brought forth,*
*Or ever You had formed the earth and the world,*
*Even from everlasting to everlasting, You are God.*

PSALM 90:2

# Thankfulness

EVER SINCE THE FIRST THANKSGIVING—WHEN THE PILGRIMS and Native Americans feasted together on turkey, venison, and popcorn—the holiday has been celebrated every year in New England. Each state set aside a day for the feast, though the dates differed from state to state.

In the 1840s, Sarah Josepha Hale, the editor of the prominent women's magazine *Godey's Lady's Book*, began campaigning to make Thanksgiving a nationally recognized holiday. She wrote to five different presidents over a period of seventeen years before one of them was convinced of the merits of her plan. On September 28, 1863, she wrote to President Abraham Lincoln, suggesting that the "day of our annual Thanksgiving [be] made a National and fixed Union Festival."[48]

Abraham Lincoln supported the legislation; Thanksgiving Day was declared a national holiday on October 3, 1863. The official proclamation read, in part:

> I do therefore invite my fellow citizens in every part of the United States, and also those who are at sea and those who are sojourning in foreign lands, to set apart and observe the last Thursday of November next, as a day of Thanksgiving and Praise to our beneficent Father who dwelleth in the Heavens.[49]

*Every good gift and every perfect gift is from above, and comes down from the Father of lights, with whom there is no variation or shadow of turning.*

JAMES 1:17

*And let the peace of God rule in your hearts, to which also you were called in one body; and be thankful. . . . And whatever you do in word or deed, do all in the name of the Lord Jesus, giving thanks to God the Father through Him.*

COLOSSIANS 3:15, 17

*Give to the* LORD, *O families of the peoples,*
*Give to the* LORD *glory and strength.*
*Give to the* LORD *the glory due His name;*
*Bring an offering, and come before Him.*
*Oh, worship the* LORD *in the beauty of holiness!*

I CHRONICLES 16:28–29

# Truth

JOHN 17:17 SAYS OF THE LORD, "YOUR WORD IS TRUTH." THIS IS true not just of each individual word, but of each concept and premise communicated in the Word of God. Few have grasped this fact as well as Harriet Beecher Stowe. And no one could hinder her in expressing truth as she understood it.

Credited by many with being the final catalyst to the Civil War, Harriet's book *Uncle Tom's Cabin* literally changed her world. She did not separate her faith from the rest of life, nor did she compartmentalize her convictions. For Harriet, God's Word was truth and the only source acceptable for determining right and wrong, just and unjust.

Many of our Founding Fathers credited God's Word as their guiding force when setting in place the ruling statutes of our nation. Truly, in our nation mercy and truth have joined through the efforts of Harriet Beecher Stowe and others like her, who are led forth by the only truth, the Word of God.

*So shall I keep Your law continually,*
*Forever and ever.*
*And I will walk at liberty,*
*For I seek Your precepts.*
*I will speak of Your testimonies also before kings,*
*And will not be ashamed.*

PSALM 119:44–46

*But the wisdom that is from above is first pure, then peaceable, gentle, willing to yield, full of mercy and good fruits, without partiality and without hypocrisy. Now the fruit of righteousness is sown in peace by those who make peace.*

JAMES 3:17–18

*He who has My commandments and keeps them, it is he who loves Me. And he who loves Me will be loved by My Father, and I will love him and manifest Myself to him.*

JOHN 14:21

# Staying True

CONSIDERED ONE OF THE GREATEST ORATORS IN AMERICAN history, Daniel Webster (1782–1852) served as a US congressman and senator as well as secretary of state for three different presidents. The following is from a speech given before the Historical Society of New York on February 23, 1852:

> If we, and our posterity, shall be true to the Christian religion, if we, and they, shall live always in the fear of God and shall respect His commandments, if we, and they, shall maintain just moral sentiments, and such conscientious convictions of duty as shall control the heart and life, we may have the highest hopes of the future fortunes of our country. . . .
>
> But, if we and our posterity reject religious institutions and authority, violate the rules of eternal justice, trifle with the injunctions of morality, and recklessly destroy the political constitution, which holds us together, no man can tell how sudden a catastrophe may overwhelm us.[50]

*To do righteousness and justice*
*Is more acceptable to the LORD than sacrifice.*
PROVERBS 21:3

*He who follows righteousness and mercy*
*Finds life, righteousness, and honor.*
PROVERBS 21:21

*He who has a generous eye will be blessed,*
*For he gives of his bread to the poor.*
PROVERBS 22:9

*My son, if your heart is wise,*
*My heart will rejoice—indeed, I myself;*
*Yes, my inmost being will rejoice*
*When your lips speak right things.*
PROVERBS 23:15–16

# "The Word and the Works of God"

BENJAMIN SILLIMAN (1779–1864), AN AMERICAN PHYSICIST, chemist, and geologist, founded and edited the *American Journal of Science and Arts*. Hear his perspective on science and Scripture:

> The relation of geology as well as astronomy to the Bible, when both are well understood, is that of perfect harmony. The Bible no where limits the age of the globe, while its chronology assigns a recent origin to the human race; and geology . . . confirms . . . that the Genesis presents a true statement of the progress of the terrestrial arrangements and of the introduction of living beings in the order in which their fossil remains are found entombed in the strata.
>
> The Word and the works of God cannot be in conflict, and the more they are studied, the more perfect will their harmony appear.[51]

*In the beginning was the Word, and the Word was with God, and the Word was God. He was in the beginning with God. All things were made through Him, and without Him nothing was made that was made.*

JOHN 1:1–3

*And the Word became flesh and dwelt among us, and we beheld His glory, the glory as of the only begotten of the Father, full of grace and truth.*

JOHN 1:14

*Let the word of Christ dwell in you richly in all wisdom, teaching and admonishing one another in psalms and hymns and spiritual songs, singing with grace in your hearts to the Lord. And whatever you do in word or deed, do all in the name of the Lord Jesus, giving thanks to God the Father through Him.*

COLOSSIANS 3:16–17

# Godly Leaders

SCRIPTURE'S UNIFYING THEME IS GOD'S UNCHANGING COVENANT with His people. When Israel stayed true to God's Word and His will, He blessed the nation with prosperity. When the people disobeyed God, they faced some stiff consequences. Then in Nehemiah 9, after Ezra read the law, the people confessed their sin and boldly reaffirmed their loyalty to God's covenant.

On March 4, 1933, in his first inaugural address and during the Great Depression, President Franklin D. Roosevelt spoke a bold word of encouragement to his fellow citizens: "Let me assert my firm belief that the only thing we have to fear is fear itself. . . . We face the arduous days that lie before us in the warm courage of the national unity; with the clear consciousness of seeking old and precious moral values."[52] Beseeching God's blessing, the president added, "May He protect each and every one of us! May He guide me in the days to come!" FDR's leadership would be a decisive factor in keeping America's resolve strong throughout the years of the Depression and the world war that followed.

*He who walks righteously and speaks uprightly,*
*He who despises the gain of oppressions,*
*Who gestures with his hands, refusing bribes,*
*Who stops his ears from hearing of bloodshed,*
*And shuts his eyes from seeing evil:*
*He will dwell on high;*
*His place of defense will be the fortress of rocks;*
*Bread will be given him,*
*His water will be sure.*

ISAIAH 33:15–16

*For this is God,*
*Our God forever and ever;*
*He will be our guide*
*Even to death.*

PSALM 48:14

*I will instruct you and teach you in the way you*
*should go;*
*I will guide you with My eye.*

PSALM 32:8

# "The Loving Devotion of a Free People"

IN HIS INAUGURAL ADDRESS ON MARCH 5, 1877, RUTHERFORD B. Hayes, the nineteenth president of the United States (1877–1881), stated the following:

> Looking for the guidance of that Divine Hand by which the destinies of nations and individuals are shaped, I call upon you, Senators, Representatives, judges, fellow-citizens, here and everywhere, to unite with me in an earnest effort to secure to our country the blessings, not only of material property, but of justice, peace, and union—a union depending not upon the constraint of force but upon the loving devotion of a free people; and that all things may be so ordered and settled upon the best and surest foundations that peace and happiness, truth and justice, religion and piety, may be established among us for all generations.[53]

*The* Lord *bless you and keep you;*
*The* Lord *make His face shine upon you,*
*And be gracious to you;*
*The* Lord *lift up His countenance upon you,*
*And give you peace.*

NUMBERS 6:24–26

*Let my cry come before You, O* Lord*;*
*Give me understanding according to Your word.*
*Let my supplication come before You;*
*Deliver me according to Your word. . . .*
*Let Your hand become my help,*
*For I have chosen Your precepts.*

PSALM 119:169–170, 173

*Establish Your word to Your servant,*
*Who is devoted to fearing You.*
*Turn away my reproach which I dread,*
*For Your judgments are good.*
*Behold, I long for Your precepts;*
*Revive me in Your righteousness.*

PSALM 119:38–40

# Guarding Truth

IN COLOSSIANS—PERHAPS THE MOST CHRIST-CENTERED BOOK in the Bible—the apostle Paul refuted a threatening heresy that devalued Christ by explaining that believers are risen with Christ and are to put off the old man and put on the new, which will result in holiness in all relationships. Paul stressed the preeminence of Christ and the completeness of the salvation He provides. Paul countered false teaching with his presentation of Jesus. A proper view of Christ is always the most powerful antidote to heresy.

Just as the Colossians needed to guard the truth of the gospel, so we need to guard our country. President Calvin Coolidge (1872–1933) said:

> The issues of the world must be met and met squarely. The forces of evil do not disdain preparation, they are always prepared and always preparing. . . . The welfare of America, the cause of civilization will forever require the contribution, of some part of the life, of all our citizens, to the natural, the necessary, and the inevitable demand for the defense of the right and the truth.[54]

*Now you yourselves are to put off all these: anger, wrath, malice, blasphemy, filthy language out of your mouth. Do not lie to one another, since you have put off the old man with his deeds, and have put on the new man who is renewed in knowledge according to the image of Him who created him, where there is neither Greek nor Jew, circumcised nor uncircumcised, barbarian, Scythian, slave nor free, but Christ is all and in all.*

COLOSSIANS 3:8–11

*I am the way, the truth, and the life. No one comes to the Father except through Me. If you had known Me, you would have known My Father also; and from now on you know Him and have seen Him.*

JOHN 14:6–7

*Sanctify them by Your truth. Your word is truth. As You sent Me into the world, I also have sent them into the world. And for their sakes I sanctify Myself, that they also may be sanctified by the truth.*

JOHN 17:17–19

# Freedom's Cost

A WISE PERSON ONCE SAID, "FREEDOM IS NEVER FREE."

Nathan Hale (1755–1776) was a schoolteacher when the Revolutionary War broke out in April 1775. After hearing about the siege of Boston, Hale joined his five brothers in the fight for independence.

Hale fought under General George Washington in New York as British General William Howe began a military buildup on Long Island. When Washington asked for a volunteer to spy behind enemy lines, Hale stepped forward. For a week he gathered information on the position of British troops, but he was captured while returning. Because of the incriminating papers Hale possessed, the British knew he was a spy. Howe ordered the twenty-year-old Hale to be hanged the following day without a trial.

Patriot Nathan Hale was hanged on September 22, 1776. Before he gave his life for his country, he made a short speech, ending with these famous and inspiring words: "I only regret that I have but one life to lose for my country."[55]

As John Adams said, "You will never know, how much it has cost the present Generation, to preserve your Freedom! I hope you will make good Use of it."[56] We must do all we can to protect the freedoms that generations past have entrusted to us.

*This is My commandment, that you love one another as I have loved you. Greater love has no one than this, than to lay down one's life for his friends.*

JOHN 15:12–13

*Happy is he who has the God of Jacob for his help,*
*Whose hope is in the* LORD *his God,*
*Who made heaven and earth,*
*The sea, and all that is in them;*
*Who keeps truth forever,*
*Who executes justice for the oppressed,*
*Who gives food to the hungry.*
*The* LORD *gives freedom to the prisoners.*

PSALM 146:5–7

*What then shall we say to these things? If God is for us, who can be against us? He who did not spare His own Son, but delivered Him up for us all, how shall He not with Him also freely give us all things?*

ROMANS 8:31–32

# The Joy of Worship

THE BOOK OF PSALMS IS A PROFOUNDLY RICH AND PERSONAL guide to worship, praise, prayer, meditation, and even instruction about God. Containing some of the most beautiful poetry ever penned, the Psalms can help us express our deepest needs, thoughts, and desires to our heavenly Father—in times of great joy as well as in times of great sorrow.

Fanny Crosby (1820–1915), one of America's most beloved hymn writers, no doubt received much inspiration and tutoring in song from time spent in the book of Psalms. Blind from infancy, she nevertheless went on to pen more than eight thousand songs of praise to God, including such classic hymns as "Near the Cross," "Praise Him, Praise Him," and "To God Be the Glory." The chorus of one of her most well-known hymns, "Blessed Assurance," sums up the theme of Psalms:

*This is my story, this is my song,*
*Praising my Savior all the day long;*
*This is my story, this is my song,*
*Praising my Savior all the day long.*[57]

*I will praise the* L*ORD according to His righteousness,*
*And will sing praise to the name of the* L*ORD*
*Most High.*

PSALM 7:17

*Oh come, let us worship and bow down;*
*Let us kneel before the* L*ORD our Maker.*
*For He is our God,*
*And we are the people of His pasture,*
*And the sheep of His hand.*

PSALM 95:6–7

*Praise the* L*ORD!*
*Praise God in His sanctuary;*
*Praise Him in His mighty firmament!*
*Praise Him for His mighty acts. . . .*
*Let everything that has breath praise the* L*ORD.*
*Praise the* L*ORD!*

PSALM 150:1–2, 6

## Common Sense

IN THE 1952 CASE *ZORACH V. CLAUSON*, THE SUPREME COURT upheld the New York City school district practice of releasing students during school hours for religious instruction:

> The First Amendment . . . does not say that, in every respect there shall be a separation of Church and State. Rather . . . there shall be no concert or union or dependency one on the other. . . . Otherwise the state and religion would be aliens to each other. . . .
>
> Municipalities would not be permitted to render police or fire protection to religious groups. . . . Prayers in our legislative halls; the appeals to the Almighty in the messages of the Chief Executive; . . . "so help me God" in our courtroom oaths . . . would be flouting the First Amendment. . . .
>
> When the state . . . cooperates with religious authorities by adjusting the schedule of public events . . . it follows the best of our traditions. For it then respects the religious nature of our people and accommodates the public service to their spiritual needs. . . . We cannot read into the Bill of Rights such a philosophy of hostility to religion.[58]

*Only take heed to yourself, and diligently keep yourself, lest you forget the things your eyes have seen, and lest they depart from your heart all the days of your life. And teach them to your children and your grandchildren.*

DEUTERONOMY 4:9

*And these words which I command you today shall be in your heart. You shall teach them diligently to your children, and shall talk of them when you sit in your house, when you walk by the way, when you lie down, and when you rise up. You shall bind them as a sign on your hand, and they shall be as frontlets between your eyes. You shall write them on the doorposts of your house and on your gates.*

DEUTERONOMY 6:6–9

*Teach me Your way, O LORD,*<br>
*And lead me in a smooth path, because of*<br>
*my enemies.*

PSALM 27:11

# Promised Blessings

AMERICA'S RICH HISTORY IS FILLED WITH ACCOUNTS OF men and women who left the comfort and familiarity of their homes and families in search of greater freedom and opportunity. With hearts set on adventure, these early pioneers braved hardships and hazards to claim their personal "promised land." And that choice required courage, determination, and faith in God.

The book of Numbers recounts a similar grand adventure, of God preparing His own people to conquer the land of milk and honey that He had promised them generations earlier. Before they could succeed, however, the people of Israel had to deal with the fear and doubt that gripped them. God required—and He requires it today—that those called by His name put their faith in Him alone. Numbers shows the process by which He brought His people to that place of trust and led them into a place of blessing.

*Trust in the* LORD *with all your heart,*
*And lean not on your own understanding;*
*In all your ways acknowledge Him,*
*And He shall direct your paths.*

PROVERBS 3:5–6

*And it shall come to pass*
*That just as you were a curse among the nations,*
*O house of Judah and house of Israel,*
*So I will save you, and you shall be a blessing.*
*Do not fear,*
*Let your hands be strong.*

ZECHARIAH 8:13

*Blessed is the man*
*Who walks not in the counsel of the ungodly,*
*Nor stands in the path of sinners,*
*Nor sits in the seat of the scornful;*
*But his delight is in the law of the* LORD,
*And in His law he meditates day and night.*

PSALM 1:1–2

# Honor the Creator

THE FOURTH PRESIDENT OF THE UNITED STATES AND "CHIEF Architect of the Constitution," James Madison (1751–1836), wrote the following:

> The Religion then of every man must be left to the conviction and conscience of every man; and it is the right of every man to exercise it as these may dictate. This right is in its nature an unalienable right. It is unalienable, because the opinions of men, depending only on the evidence contemplated by their own minds cannot follow the dictates of other men: It is unalienable also, because what is here a right towards men, is a duty towards the Creator. It is the duty of every man to render to the Creator such homage and such only as he believes to be acceptable to him. This duty is precedent, both in order of time and in degree of obligation, to the claims of Civil Society. Before any man can be considered as a member of Civil Society, he must be considered as a subject of the Governor of the Universe.[59]

*Remember now your Creator in the days of your*
*youth,*
*Before the difficult days come,*
*And the years draw near when you say,*
*"I have no pleasure in them."*

ECCLESIASTES 12:1

*Have you not known?*
*Have you not heard?*
*The everlasting God, the* LORD*,*
*The Creator of the ends of the earth,*
*Neither faints nor is weary.*
*His understanding is unsearchable.*
*He gives power to the weak,*
*And to those who have no might He increases*
*strength.*

ISAIAH 40:28–29

*Therefore let those who suffer according to the will of God commit their souls to Him in doing good, as to a faithful Creator.*

I PETER 4:19

# The Fundamentals

IN THE LATE NINETEENTH AND EARLY TWENTIETH CENTURIES, conservative evangelical Christians began to reject the growing influence of modernism, especially the movement toward a social, humanistic gospel. Relying on *The Fundamentals*, written by prominent pastors and scholars in the 1910s, these believers affirmed Christian beliefs being questioned by growing liberalism.

The first formulation of these beliefs can be traced to the Niagara Bible Conference. In 1910, the General Assembly of the Presbyterian Church outlined "five fundamentals":

1. Inerrancy of the Scriptures
2. The virgin birth and the deity of Jesus Christ (Isaiah 7:14)
3. The doctrine of substitutionary atonement by God's grace and through human faith (Hebrews 9)
4. The bodily resurrection of Jesus (Matthew 28)
5. The authenticity of Christ's miracles[60]

Many strongly conservative churches combined their religious views with social and political action. The movement's plain and powerful teaching revived the American church. These efforts remain a major force in religious America.

*I am the true vine, and My Father is the vinedresser. Every branch in Me that does not bear fruit He takes away; and every branch that bears fruit He prunes, that it may bear more fruit. . . .*

*I am the vine, you are the branches. He who abides in Me, and I in him, bears much fruit; for without Me you can do nothing.*

JOHN 15:1–2, 5

*Finally, brethren, whatever things are true, whatever things are noble, whatever things are just, whatever things are pure, whatever things are lovely, whatever things are of good report, if there is any virtue and if there is anything praiseworthy—meditate on these things. The things which you learned and received and heard and saw in me, these do, and the God of peace will be with you.*

PHILIPPIANS 4:8–9

# As for Me!

PATRICK HENRY (1736–1799) WAS ONE OF THE MOST PASSIONATE and fiery advocates of the American Revolution. Many have compared him to an Old Testament prophet in his powerful denunciations of corruption in government officials and his defense of the colonists' rights. Elected to the Virginia legislature in 1775, he rallied Virginia into military preparedness.

Rebellion against unjust taxes had begun, and the British had posted troops throughout the colonies and warships in the harbors. On March 23, 1775, during the Second Virginia Convention's debates on whether to declare independence or negotiate with the British, Patrick Henry called upon his countrymen to trust God:

> Sir, we shall not fight our battles alone. There is a just God who presides over the destinies of nations, and who will raise up friends to fight our battles for us. The battle, sir, is not to the strong alone; it is to the vigilant, the active, the brave.[61]

Hear his passionate conclusion:

> Is life so dear, or peace so sweet, as to be purchased at the price of chains and slavery? Forbid it, Almighty God! I know not what course others may take; but as for me, give me liberty or give me death![62]

*Choose for yourselves this day whom you will serve, whether the gods which your fathers served that were on the other side of the River, or the gods of the Amorites, in whose land you dwell. But as for me and my house, we will serve the* LORD.

JOSHUA 24:15

*Therefore, having been justified by faith, we have peace with God through our Lord Jesus Christ, through whom also we have access by faith into this grace in which we stand, and rejoice in hope of the glory of God.*

ROMANS 5:1–2

*You did not choose Me, but I chose you and appointed you that you should go and bear fruit, and that your fruit should remain, that whatever you ask the Father in My name He may give you. These things I command you, that you love one another.*

JOHN 15:16–17

# Perseverance

TIME AND CHANCE BRING UNEXPECTED CIRCUMSTANCE—sometimes glorious, sometimes agonizing, but always unforeseen. No matter their skill, wealth, or wisdom, all people face trials and all must choose how to respond.

Jarena Lee was a woman who knew what it meant to persevere. Born in 1783, when women were strongly encouraged to remain silently submissive, Jarena felt called to preach the Word of God. Being a woman was a hindrance; being a free Black woman seemed to bar her way at every turn. But with a strong faith and unstoppable determination, Jarena became the first woman authorized to preach in the African Methodist Episcopal Church.[63] She kept moving forward toward the destiny God had prepared.

The value of perseverance is made clear in Paul's words to the Romans: "We also glory in tribulations, knowing that tribulation produces perseverance; and perseverance, character; and character, hope" (Romans 5:3–4). This is a progression spurred on by time and chance. It is a progression that has been lived out in undeniable ways in the women of our nation.

*These all died in faith, not having received the promises, but having seen them afar off were assured of them, embraced them and confessed that they were strangers and pilgrims on the earth. . . . Therefore God is not ashamed to be called their God, for He has prepared a city for them.*

HEBREWS 11:13, 16

*Those who wait on the Lord*
*Shall renew their strength;*
*They shall mount up with wings like eagles,*
*They shall run and not be weary,*
*They shall walk and not faint.*

ISAIAH 40:31

*Therefore, my beloved brethren, be steadfast, immovable, always abounding in the work of the Lord, knowing that your labor is not in vain in the Lord.*

I CORINTHIANS 15:58

# Our Sacred Duty

ACCORDING TO THE DECLARATION OF INDEPENDENCE, THE American colonists were determined to defend "the Laws of Nature and of Nature's God."[64] This phrase defines the key principle upon which the Founders stood. The "laws of nature" meant the will of God for man as revealed to man's reason. However, because man is fallen and his reason does not always comprehend this law, God gave us the Bible to make His law absolutely clear.

The churches in the colonies became a voice of freedom, stirring the fires of liberty by telling the colonists that the British government was usurping their God-given rights and that the king and Parliament were violating the laws of God. The Founding Fathers were convinced that it was their sacred duty to start a revolution in order to uphold the law of God against the unjust and oppressive laws of men. This fight for political liberty was seen as a sacred cause because civil liberty is an inalienable right, according to God's natural law.

*You shall walk after the* L*ORD your God and fear Him, and keep His commandments and obey His voice; you shall serve Him and hold fast to Him.*

DEUTERONOMY 13:4

*For this is the will of God, that by doing good you may put to silence the ignorance of foolish men—as free, yet not using liberty as a cloak for vice, but as bondservants of God. Honor all people. Love the brotherhood. Fear God. Honor the king.*

1 PETER 2:15–17

*But you are a chosen generation, a royal priesthood, a holy nation, His own special people, that you may proclaim the praises of Him who called you out of darkness into His marvelous light; who once were not a people but are now the people of God, who had not obtained mercy but now have obtained mercy.*

1 PETER 2:9–10

# Justice

THE TERM *JUSTICE* OFTEN BRINGS TO MIND THE QUESTION OF fairness: Is the result or consequence impartial and equitable for all? Yet, perspective may dictate one's answer to this question. For the human race, true justice seems ever-elusive; a human mind is too limited and easily swayed to truly define and uphold pure, untainted justice.

At the heart of genuine justice lies a love that cannot discriminate. Pure, impartial justice necessitates the recognition of equal worth and a loyalty to humanity, not to a cause. Justice in all its complexity requires a greater mind and a greater heart than any man or woman can claim. Only God can determine the course of true justice. Those who listen for His leading show to the world the superior quality of a justice that is God-inspired.

Coretta Scott King once said, "Freedom and justice cannot be parceled out in pieces to suit political convenience. . . . I don't believe you can stand for freedom for one group of people and deny it to others."[65] At the heart of this quote lies an understanding of true justice. It is founded in love and upheld by truth. It is a reflection of the heart of God.

*For the* L*ORD is a God of justice;*
*Blessed are all those who wait for Him. . . .*
*He will be very gracious to you at the sound of*
*your cry;*
*When He hears it, He will answer you.*

ISAIAH 30:18–19

*Thus says the* L*ORD: "Execute judgment and righteousness, and deliver the plundered out of the hand of the oppressor. Do no wrong and do no violence to the stranger, the fatherless, or the widow, nor shed innocent blood in this place."*

JEREMIAH 22:3

*He has shown you, O man, what is good;*
*And what does the* L*ORD require of you*
*But to do justly,*
*To love mercy,*
*And to walk humbly with your God?*

MICAH 6:8

# Forgetting God

IN ANGUISH OVER THE RAVAGES OF CIVIL WAR, PRESIDENT Abraham Lincoln declared a National Fast Day on March 30, 1863:

> We have been the recipients of the choicest bounties of Heaven; we have been preserved these many years in peace and prosperity; we have grown in numbers, wealth, and power as no other nation has ever grown. But we have forgotten God. We have forgotten the gracious hand which preserved us in peace and multiplied and enriched and strengthened us, and we have vainly imagined, in the deceitfulness of our hearts, that all these blessings were produced by some superior wisdom and virtue of our own. Intoxicated with unbroken success, we have become too self-sufficient to feel the necessity of redeeming and preserving grace, too proud to pray to the God that made us.
>
> It behooves us, then, to humble ourselves before the offended Power, to confess our national sins, and to pray for clemency and forgiveness.[66]

*The humble He guides in justice,*
*And the humble He teaches His way.*
*All the paths of the* L*ORD* *are mercy and truth,*
*To such as keep His covenant and His testimonies.*

PSALM 25:9–10

*For I know the thoughts that I think toward you, says the* L*ORD*, *thoughts of peace and not of evil, to give you a future and a hope. Then you will call upon Me and go and pray to Me, and I will listen to you. And you will seek Me and find Me, when you search for Me with all your heart.*

JEREMIAH 29:11–13

*If we say that we have no sin, we deceive ourselves, and the truth is not in us. If we confess our sins, He is faithful and just to forgive us our sins and to cleanse us from all unrighteousness.*

I JOHN 1:8–9

# Shield of Strength

CAPTAIN RUSSELL RIPPETOE WAS SERVING IN OPERATION IRAQI Freedom in March 2003. Previously, while serving in Afghanistan, Rippetoe saw men die, which brought a renewal to his Christian faith and a new passion for the Bible. On the chain around his neck, he wore a "Shield of Strength," a one-by-two-inch emblem displaying a US flag on one side and words from Joshua 1:9 on the other.

On April 3, 2003, Rippetoe's company was manning a nighttime checkpoint near the Hadithah Dam when a vehicle approached. Suddenly, a woman jumped out and cried, "I'm hungry. I need food and water!" Protecting his men, Rippetoe gave the order to hold back as he moved toward the woman to see how he could help. When she hesitated, the driver detonated a car bomb that killed Captain Rippetoe, Sergeant Nino Livaudais, and Specialist Ryan Long and wounded two others.

Rippetoe believed the ancient words of Joshua 1:9: "The LORD your God is with you wherever you go." Rippetoe, who died trying to help someone, was the first casualty of the Iraq conflict to be buried at Arlington National Cemetery.[67]

*The LORD is my light and my salvation;*
*Whom shall I fear?*

PSALM 27:1

*For His anger is but for a moment,*
*His favor is for life;*
*Weeping may endure for a night,*
*But joy comes in the morning.*

PSALM 30:5

*The LORD is my strength and my shield;*
*My heart trusted in Him, and I am helped;*
*Therefore my heart greatly rejoices,*
*And with my song I will praise Him.*

PSALM 28:7

# Praying for the Legislature

WARREN EARL BURGER, CHIEF JUSTICE OF THE US SUPREME Court from 1969 to 1986, delivered the court's opinion in the 1983 case *Marsh v. Chambers*, regarding chaplains opening legislative sessions with prayer:

> Clearly the men who wrote the First Amendment Religion Clause did not view paid legislative chaplains and opening prayers as a violation of that Amendment. . . .
>
> It can hardly be thought that, in the same week, Members of the First Congress voted to appoint and pay a chaplain for each House and also voted to approve the draft of the First Amendment . . . [that] they intended . . . to forbid what they had just declared acceptable.[68]

In 1980 Judge Warren Keith Urbom from Nebraska said this:

> The legislature by majority vote invites a clergyman to give a prayer, neither the inviting nor the giving nor the hearing of the prayer is making a law. On this basis alone . . . the sayings of prayers, per se, in the legislative halls at the opening session is not prohibited by the First and Fourteenth Amendments.[69]

*Give heed to the voice of my cry,*
*My King and my God,*
*For to You I will pray.*
*My voice You shall hear in the morning, O LORD;*
*In the morning I will direct it to You,*
*And I will look up.*

PSALM 5:2–3

*Be anxious for nothing, but in everything by prayer and supplication, with thanksgiving, let your requests be made known to God; and the peace of God, which surpasses all understanding, will guard your hearts and minds through Christ Jesus.*

PHILIPPIANS 4:6–7

*Let every soul be subject to the governing authorities. For there is no authority except from God, and the authorities that exist are appointed by God.*

ROMANS 13:1

# Following Christ's Example

BENJAMIN FRANKLIN BUTLER (1795–1858), US ATTORNEY General under President Andrew Jackson, knew the value of God's Word:

> He is truly happy, whatever may be his temporal condition, who can call God his father, in the full assurance of faith and hope. And amid all his trials, and conflicts, and doubts, the feeblest Christian is still comparatively happy, because cheered by the hope . . . that the hour is coming when he shall be delivered from "this body of sin and death," and in the vision of his Redeemer . . . approximate to the . . . felicity of angels. . . .
>
> Not only does [the Bible] inculcate, with sanctions of the highest import, a system of the purest morality, but in the person and character of our blessed Savior it exhibits a tangible illustration of that system.
>
> In Him we have set before us . . . a model of feeling and action, adapted to all times, places, and circumstances; and combining so much of wisdom, benevolence, and holiness, that none can fathom its sublimity, and yet presented in a form so simple that even a child may be made to understand, and taught to love it.[70]

*Now thanks be to God who always leads us in triumph in Christ, and through us diffuses the fragrance of His knowledge in every place. For we are to God the fragrance of Christ among those who are being saved and among those who are perishing.*

2 CORINTHIANS 2:14–15

*Brethren, if a man is overtaken in any trespass, you who are spiritual restore such a one in a spirit of gentleness, considering yourself lest you also be tempted. Bear one another's burdens, and so fulfill the law of Christ.*

GALATIANS 6:1–2

*Brethren, I do not count myself to have apprehended; but one thing I do, forgetting those things which are behind and reaching forward to those things which are ahead, I press toward the goal for the prize of the upward call of God in Christ Jesus.*

PHILIPPIANS 3:13–14

# Building Character and Lives

ADVISER TO PRESIDENTS ROOSEVELT AND TAFT, EDUCATOR

Booker T. Washington (1856–1915) founded Tuskegee Institute, a vocational school for Black Americans. Its graduates became leaders and educators across the nation.

Born into slavery, Washington worked in Virginia coal mines and salt furnaces from age nine. Determined to get an education, at sixteen he went to Hampton Institute, an industrial school for Black Americans. Graduating with honors in just three years, he joined the faculty and was soon asked to lead a new school in Tuskegee. Starting with an abandoned church, he built Tuskegee Institute into a school of 107 buildings with over fifteen hundred students and more than two hundred teachers and professors—all by 1915.

Wanting to produce businessmen, farmers, and teachers, Washington offered traditional academic courses; industry and trade skills like bricklaying, forestry, sewing, cooking, and agriculture; and the training of "head, hand, and heart," an emphasis on high moral character shaped by the Christian faith. Washington wrote that "the Christlike work which the Church of all denominations in America has done" convinced him of the value of the Christian life.[71]

*He who follows righteousness and mercy*
*Finds life, righteousness, and honor.*

PROVERBS 21:21

*For we are God's fellow workers; you are God's field, you are God's building. According to the grace of God which was given to me, as a wise master builder I have laid the foundation, and another builds on it. But let each one take heed how he builds on it. For no other foundation can anyone lay than that which is laid, which is Jesus Christ.*

1 CORINTHIANS 3:9–11

*Therefore, if anyone is in Christ, he is a new creation; old things have passed away; behold, all things have become new. Now all things are of God, who has reconciled us to Himself through Jesus Christ, and has given us the ministry of reconciliation, that is, that God was in Christ reconciling the world to Himself, not imputing their trespasses to them, and has committed to us the word of reconciliation.*

2 CORINTHIANS 5:17–19

# A Godly Legacy

AT AGE SIX, HENRY JOHN HEINZ (1844–1919) HELPED HIS MOTHER tend a small family garden. At twelve, he was working more than three acres and making deliveries to Pittsburgh grocery stores. He went on to found a company that he named 57 Varieties. In 2015 the H. J. Heinz Company merged with Kraft Foods to become the fifth-largest food and beverage company in the world.[72]

Heinz's company pioneered safe and sanitary food preparation and was ahead of its time in employee relations, providing free medical benefits. Women held supervisory positions. Henry Heinz was also very involved in promoting Sunday school in Pittsburgh and around the world.

In his will, Heinz said, "I desire to set forth at the very beginning of this will . . . a confession of my faith in Jesus Christ as my Saviour. I also desire to bear witness to the fact that throughout my life . . . I have been wonderfully sustained by my faith in God through Jesus Christ. This legacy was left me by my consecrated mother, a woman of strong faith, and to it I attribute any success I may have attained during my life."[73]

*Fear not, for I am with you;*
*Be not dismayed, for I am your God.*
*I will strengthen you,*
*Yes, I will help you,*
*I will uphold you with My righteous right hand.*

ISAIAH 41:10

*Blessed are you when they revile and persecute you, and say all kinds of evil against you falsely for My sake. Rejoice and be exceedingly glad, for great is your reward in heaven, for so they persecuted the prophets who were before you.*

MATTHEW 5:11–12

*Let your light so shine before men, that they may see your good works and glorify your Father in heaven.*

MATTHEW 5:16

# Obeying God

PERHAPS SURPRISINGLY, NEW ENGLAND MINISTERS PLAYED A key role in rallying popular support for war against England. They pressed their congregations to overthrow King George because they believed that rebellion to tyrants was obedience to God. From many pulpits, ministers recruited troops and strengthened them for battle.

These church leaders knew that the Bible places great emphasis on due submission to civil authorities (Romans 13), but they noted that many passages approve resistance to ungodly authority (Acts 5:29).

It is, therefore, no coincidence that one of the watchwords of the American Revolution was "No King But King Jesus."[74] Most of the patriots found in their faith and in God's Word the courage to risk their lives and properties in order to break the tyranny of an unjust human authority. According to their Christian worldview, obedience to God took precedence over loyalty to country or government: Their primary allegiance was to the Lord Jesus Christ.

*Now it shall come to pass, if you diligently obey the voice of the LORD your God, to observe carefully all His commandments which I command you today, that the LORD your God will set you high above all nations of the earth. And all these blessings shall come upon you and overtake you, because you obey the voice of the LORD your God.*

DEUTERONOMY 28:1–2

*But this is what I commanded them, saying, "Obey My voice, and I will be your God, and you shall be My people. And walk in all the ways that I have commanded you, that it may be well with you."*

JEREMIAH 7:23

*But Peter and the other apostles answered and said: "We ought to obey God rather than men. The God of our fathers raised up Jesus whom you murdered by hanging on a tree. Him God has exalted to His right hand to be Prince and Savior, to give repentance to Israel and forgiveness of sins."*

ACTS 5:29–31

# The Goal from the Start

THE FIRST PERMANENT SETTLEMENT IN THE NEW WORLD WAS the English colony established in 1607 at Jamestown, Virginia. Similar to the other colonial charters, the First Charter of Virginia emphasized the Christian character of the colonists' purpose:

> We, greatly commending, and graciously accepting of, their Desires for the Furtherance of so noble a Work, which may, by the Providence of Almighty God, hereafter tend to the Glory of His Divine Majesty, in propagating of Christian Religion to such people, as yet live in Darkness and miserable Ignorance of the true Knowledge and Worship of God.[75]

Similarly, in 1620, the Pilgrims established a colony at Plymouth, Massachusetts. Their purpose was to establish a political commonwealth governed by biblical standards. The Mayflower Compact, their initial governing document, clearly stated that what they had undertaken was for "the Glory of God, and Advancement of the Christian Faith."[76] William Bradford, the second governor of Plymouth, said, "[The colonists cherished] a great hope and inward zeal . . . of laying some good foundation . . . for the propagating and advancing of the gospel of the kingdom of Christ in those remote parts of the world."[77]

*Go therefore and make disciples of all the nations, baptizing them in the name of the Father and of the Son and of the Holy Spirit, teaching them to observe all things that I have commanded you; and lo, I am with you always, even to the end of the age. Amen.*

MATTHEW 28:19–20

*For I am not ashamed of the gospel of Christ, for it is the power of God to salvation for everyone who believes, for the Jew first and also for the Greek.*

ROMANS 1:16

*Truly my soul silently waits for God;*
*From Him comes my salvation.*
*He only is my rock and my salvation;*
*He is my defense;*
*I shall not be greatly moved.*

PSALM 62:1–2

# Love

OF ALL THE TOPICS IN SCRIPTURE, LOVE IS THE GREATEST. THE reason is as simple as it is profound: "God is love" (1 John 4:8). Love is not simply an attribute of God; it is not just a feeling of warmth and tenderness that flows from Him toward us. Love is the very energy of God. He is its source and its definition.

In an attempt to communicate the nature of love, the apostle Paul penned 1 Corinthians 13:1–8. He describes love as kind, long-suffering, humble, peaceful, and undying. In doing so, he makes it clear that love is the flowing of the very essence of God in and through our lives.

In the life of Dorothy Walker Bush, we see a picture of faith-anchored, hope-filled love. In raising her children, she challenged them and encouraged them. She sought to instill in them equal amounts of self-worth and self-sacrifice. In doing so, she influenced two future presidents—her son and grandson—who, in turn, influenced a nation.

Love that finds its source in the Author of love is an unstoppable force that infuses all it touches with compassion and empathy. May this very unstoppable force flood our land; and may we, in turn, be a channel of that love to the world.

*And above all things have fervent love for one another, for "love will cover a multitude of sins." Be hospitable to one another without grumbling. As each one has received a gift, minister it to one another, as good stewards of the manifold grace of God.*

I PETER 4:8–10

*A new commandment I give to you, that you love one another; as I have loved you, that you also love one another. By this all will know that you are My disciples, if you have love for one another.*

JOHN 13:34–35

*Beloved, let us love one another, for love is of God; and everyone who loves is born of God and knows God.*

I JOHN 4:7

# Words That Bless

THE BOOK OF REVELATION UNVEILS OUR LORD JESUS CHRIST AT His second coming, the future times, and the world to come. Penned by the apostle John during his exile on the island of Patmos, Revelation centers around visions and symbols of the resurrected Christ, who alone has the authority to judge the earth, remake it, and rule it in righteousness. Revelation shows the divine plan of redemption being brought to fruition.

In the final chapter, Jesus Christ says to the apostle John, "I am the Alpha and the Omega, the Beginning and the End, the First and the Last" (22:13). There is no doubt that the risen Christ is indeed worthy to be praised and worshiped throughout eternity. It is interesting that in our nation's capital, the first and last rays of sunlight fall every day upon its tallest building—the 555-foot Washington Monument. And there on its top, inscribed on the four-sided aluminum capstone, are the Latin words *Laus Deo*, which means "Praise be to God."[78] This simple expression of praise reflects America's abiding belief that God has blessed our country with liberty and divine favor.

*I am He who lives, and was dead, and behold, I am alive forevermore. Amen. And I have the keys of Hades and of Death. Write the things which you have seen, and the things which are, and the things which will take place after this.*

REVELATION 1:18–19

*Behold, I stand at the door and knock. If anyone hears My voice and opens the door, I will come in to him and dine with him, and he with Me. To him who overcomes I will grant to sit with Me on My throne, as I also overcame and sat down with My Father on His throne.*

REVELATION 3:20–21

*Blessed are those who do His commandments, that they may have the right to the tree of life, and may enter through the gates into the city.*

REVELATION 22:14

# All in the Family

QUITE POSSIBLY, THE MOST PROFOUNDLY INFLUENTIAL WOMEN in the world are mothers. Consciously or unconsciously, for good or for ill, a mother's beliefs and actions will affect her children forever.

Morrow Graham was a mother who was remembered by her famous son, evangelist Billy Graham, as one of the best influences in his life. Morrow and her husband, Frank, raised their children on a dairy farm in North Carolina. The hours were long and the work hard, but no matter how tired they were, Morrow made sure she read the Bible and prayed with her children daily. She firmly believed that praying for her children was one of the most important things she could do for them. She also wanted them to know and love the Word of God, saying, "There was only one right way to live, and it was all laid out for us in the Bible."[79]

She promoted family solidarity, a sound work ethic, and a strong faith. With humility, she also recognized that she did not always succeed and showed her children the example of asking for forgiveness and trusting the Lord to bring good even out of her failures.

*And these words which I command you today shall be in your heart. You shall teach them diligently to your children.*

DEUTERONOMY 6:6–7

*Give ear, O my people, to my law;*
*Incline your ears to the words of my mouth.*
*We will not hide them from their children,*
*Telling to the generation to come the praises of*
*the* L*ORD*,
*And His strength and His wonderful works that He*
*has done.*

PSALM 78:1, 4

*Whoever receives one little child like this in My name receives Me. . . . Take heed that you do not despise one of these little ones, for I say to you that in heaven their angels always see the face of My Father who is in heaven.*

MATTHEW 18:5, 10

# Glorious and Pure Morality

IN THE 1844 CASE *VIDAL V. GIRARD'S EXECUTORS*, JUSTICE JOSEPH Story upheld the use of the Bible and the teaching of Christian moral principles in American education.

In this case, Girard's will permitted the teaching of the Christian religion, just not by members of the clergy. Story's opinion that Girard's will was not derogatory to the Christian religion rested on two determinations. First, a layman was capable of teaching the general principles of Christianity: "Why may not laymen instruct in the general principles of Christianity as well as ecclesiastics?"[80]

Second, Girard's will actually permitted the teaching of the Bible in the school. As Judge Story's opinion stated:

> Why may not the Bible, and especially the New Testament, without note or . . . comment be read and taught as a divine revelation . . . its general precepts expounded, its evidences explained, and its glorious principles of morality inculcated? . . . Where can the purest principles of morality be learned so clearly or so perfectly as from the New Testament? Where are benevolence, the love of truth, sobriety, and industry, so powerfully and irresistibly inculcated as in the sacred volume?[81]

*Smoke went up from His nostrils,*
*And devouring fire from His mouth;*
*Coals were kindled by it.*
*He bowed the heavens also, and came down*
*With darkness under His feet.*
*And He rode upon a cherub, and flew;*
*He flew upon the wings of the wind.*

PSALM 18:8–10

*My son, keep your father's command,*
*And do not forsake the law of your mother.*
*Bind them continually upon your heart;*
*Tie them around your neck.*
*When you roam, they will lead you;*
*When you sleep, they will keep you;*
*And when you awake, they will speak with you.*
*For the commandment is a lamp,*
*And the law a light;*
*Reproofs of instruction are the way of life.*

PROVERBS 6:20–23

# No Ordinary Claims

SIMON GREENLEAF (1783–1853) WAS THE ROYALL PROFESSOR OF Law at Harvard and is considered one of the greatest legal minds in Western history. Greenleaf examined the evidence for the resurrection, came to the conclusion that it happened, and became a believer. In his *Testimony of the Evangelists*, Greenleaf wrote:

> The religion of Jesus Christ aims at nothing less than the utter overthrow of all other systems of religion in the world; denouncing them as inadequate to the wants of man, false in their foundations, and dangerous in their tendency. . . .
>
> These are no ordinary claims; and it seems hardly possible for a rational being to regard them with even a subdued interest; much less to treat them with mere indifference and contempt. If not true, they are little else than the pretensions of a bold imposture, which, not satisfied with having already enslaved millions of the human race, seeks to continue its encroachments upon human liberty, until all nations shall be subjugated under its iron rule.
>
> But if they are well founded and just, they can be no less than the high requirements of Heaven.[82]

*Indeed the hour is coming, yes, has now come, that you will be scattered, each to his own, and will leave Me alone. And yet I am not alone, because the Father is with Me. These things I have spoken to you, that in Me you may have peace. In the world you will have tribulation; but be of good cheer, I have overcome the world.*

JOHN 16:32–33

*If you abide in Me, and My words abide in you, you will ask what you desire, and it shall be done for you. By this My Father is glorified, that you bear much fruit; so you will be My disciples.*

JOHN 15:7–8

*Let not your heart be troubled; you believe in God, believe also in Me. In My Father's house are many mansions; if it were not so, I would have told you. I go to prepare a place for you. And if I go and prepare a place for you, I will come again and receive you to Myself; that where I am, there you may be also.*

JOHN 14:1–3

# The Soul of America

HEAR THESE THOUGHTS FROM CHARLES MALIK (1906–1987), Lebanon's ambassador to the United Nations and president of the thirteenth session of the UN General Assembly in 1959:

> The good [in the United States] would never have come into being without the blessing and power of Jesus Christ. . . . Whoever tries to conceive the American word without taking full account of the suffering and love and salvation of Christ is only dreaming. I know how embarrassing this matter is to politicians, bureaucrats, businessmen, and cynics; but, whatever these honored men think, the irrefutable truth is that the soul of America is, at its best and highest, Christian.[83]

*Blessed is the nation whose God is the* L*ORD,*
*The people He has chosen as His own inheritance.*
*The* L*ORD looks from heaven;*
*He sees all the sons of men.*
*From the place of His dwelling He looks*
*On all the inhabitants of the earth;*
*He fashions their hearts individually;*
*He considers all their works.*

PSALM 33:12–15

*For I am not ashamed of the gospel of Christ, for it is the power of God to salvation for everyone who believes, for the Jew first and also for the Greek. For in it the righteousness of God is revealed from faith to faith; as it is written, "The just shall live by faith."*

ROMANS 1:16–17

# Spiritual Warfare

AFTER RECEIVING PAUL'S FIRST LETTER, THE CORINTHIAN church was swayed by false teachers who accused Paul of being proud, unimpressive, and unqualified to be an apostle of Jesus Christ. Recognizing this as spiritual war, Paul sent Titus to Corinth to address this issue.

Every believer needs to know that the opposition that comes their way has its source in evil forces that oppose God and His truth. As Paul himself wrote, "We do not wrestle against flesh and blood, but against principalities, against powers, against the rulers of the darkness of this age, against spiritual hosts of wickedness in the heavenly places" (Ephesians 6:12).

Whether they face immorality or false teaching, church leaders must take action to remedy the problem. The same is true of government. President Thomas Jefferson stated, "When once a republic is corrupted, there is no possibility of remedying any of the growing evils but by removing the corruption and restoring its lost principles; every other correction is either useless or a new evil."

*For though we walk in the flesh, we do not war according to the flesh. For the weapons of our warfare are not carnal but mighty in God for pulling down strongholds, casting down arguments and every high thing that exalts itself against the knowledge of God, bringing every thought into captivity to the obedience of Christ.*

2 CORINTHIANS 10:3–5

*Finally, my brethren, be strong in the Lord and in the power of His might. Put on the whole armor of God, that you may be able to stand against the wiles of the devil. For we do not wrestle against flesh and blood, but against principalities, against powers, against the rulers of the darkness of this age, against spiritual hosts of wickedness in the heavenly places.*

EPHESIANS 6:10–12

*Therefore submit to God. Resist the devil and he will flee from you. Draw near to God and He will draw near to you. Cleanse your hands, you sinners; and purify your hearts, you double-minded.*

JAMES 4:7–8

# Victory

OUR NATION HAS KNOWN MORE THAN ITS SHARE OF TREMENdous victories in battle. Most of the wars we face, however, are of a much more personal nature. We fight against perceived wrongs and injustice. Though we may dream of becoming the victors over life's troubles and pain, the battles of this life will be constant. Jesus' very words confirm this to be true: "In the world you will have tribulation" (John 16:33). Where then is the victory?

For the people of our nation, victory has come to mean the vanquishing of an enemy. Yet true victory encompasses so much more. It is a state of security that exists regardless of circumstance. It is the recognition that triumph can only be found in God. Romans 8:37 states, "In all these things we are more than conquerors through Him who loved us." "These things" are the troubles and hardships life brings our way. Though we may not be able to avoid "these things," we can walk confidently through them, knowing that Jesus is with us through every step.

True victory is the condition of a soul at rest, trusting in God's justice and holding to His grace.

*Therefore take up the whole armor of God, that you may be able to withstand in the evil day, and having done all, to stand.*

EPHESIANS 6:13

*For whatever is born of God overcomes the world. And this is the victory that has overcome the world—our faith.*

I JOHN 5:4

*And He said to them, "I saw Satan fall like lightning from heaven. Behold, I give you the authority to trample on serpents and scorpions, and over all the power of the enemy, and nothing shall by any means hurt you. Nevertheless do not rejoice in this, that the spirits are subject to you, but rather rejoice because your names are written in heaven."*

LUKE 10:18–20

# Bible or Bayonet

CONSIDER THE BOLDNESS OF ROBERT WINTHROP, LAWYER, philanthropist, and speaker of the US House of Representatives from 1847 to 1849:

> Men may as well build their houses upon the sand and expect to see them stand, when the rains fall, and the winds blow, and the floods come, as to found free institutions upon any other basis than that of morality and virtue, of which the Word of God is the only authoritative rule. . . .
>
> All societies of men must be governed in some way or other. The less they have of stringent State Government, the more they must have of individual self-government. The less they rely on public law or physical force, the more they must rely on private moral restraint.
>
> Men, in a word, must necessarily be controlled either by a power within them, or a power without them; either by the word of God or by the strong arm of man; either by the Bible, or by the bayonet.
>
> It may do . . . other governments to talk about the State supporting religion. Here, under our own free institutions, it is Religion which must support the State.[84]

*Whoever hears these sayings of Mine, and does them, I will liken him to a wise man who built his house on the rock: and the rain descended, the floods came, and the winds blew and beat on that house; and it did not fall, for it was founded on the rock.*

MATTHEW 7:24–25

*He shall judge between many peoples,*
*And rebuke strong nations afar off;*
*They shall beat their swords into plowshares,*
*And their spears into pruning hooks;*
*Nation shall not lift up sword against nation,*
*Neither shall they learn war anymore.*
*But everyone shall sit under his vine and under his*
*fig tree,*
*And no one shall make them afraid;*
*For the mouth of the* LORD *of hosts has spoken.*

MICAH 4:3–4

# America's Fighting Preachers

IN 1776, LUTHERAN PASTOR JOHN PETER GABRIEL MUHLENBERG concluded a sermon: "In the language of holy writ, there was a time for all things, a time to preach and a time . . . to fight, and that time had now come!"[85] He then threw off his clerical robes to reveal the uniform of a Revolutionary Army officer. That afternoon, at the head of three hundred men, he marched off to join General Washington's troops and became colonel of the 8th Virginia Regiment.

Ministers turned the colonial resistance into a righteous cause not only from the pulpit, but also in state legislatures and on the battlefield, from military chaplains to taking up arms and leading troops into battle.

Ultimately, the Continental Army captured two key British armies at Saratoga in 1777 and Yorktown in 1781. That is when Patrick Henry spoke the prophetic words: "The millions of people, armed in the holy cause of liberty, and in such a country as that which we possess, are invincible by any force which our enemy can send against us."[86]

*To everything there is a season,*
*A time for every purpose under heaven. . . .*
*A time to kill,*
*And a time to heal;*
*A time to break down,*
*And a time to build up;*
*A time to love,*
*And a time to hate;*
*A time of war,*
*And a time of peace.*

ECCLESIASTES 3:1, 3, 8

*There is no fear in love; but perfect love casts out fear, because fear involves torment. But he who fears has not been made perfect in love. We love Him because He first loved us.*

I JOHN 4:18–19

# America's Bedrock

FOUNDATIONS ARE CRUCIAL TO THE SUCCESS OF ANY VENture, whether it is building a house or building a nation. When the Founding Fathers set about to establish the bedrock that would define America's greatness, they went right to the source, declaring that all human beings are "endowed by their Creator with certain unalienable Rights."[87]

The Bible contains the foundational truth that God is the Source of all life, sovereign over history, and our only hope for the peace, happiness, and true liberty we all crave. In Genesis, the "book of beginnings," we witness God's creation of heaven and earth by His powerful word, the beginnings of man's rebellion and sin, and God's calling of a covenant people through which He would bring salvation to all the peoples of the earth through His one and only Son.

*I will make you a great nation;*
*I will bless you*
*And make your name great;*
*And you shall be a blessing.*
*I will bless those who bless you,*
*And I will curse him who curses you;*
*And in you all the families of the earth shall be*
*blessed.*

GENESIS 12:2–3

*In Him also we have obtained an inheritance, being predestined according to the purpose of Him who works all things according to the counsel of His will, that we who first trusted in Christ should be to the praise of His glory.*

EPHESIANS 1:11–12

*The counsel of the LORD stands forever,*
*The plans of His heart to all generations.*
*Blessed is the nation whose God is the LORD,*
*The people He has chosen as His own inheritance.*

PSALM 33:11–12

# Spreading the Gospel

THE FOUNDING OF OUR BELOVED NATION AND THE GROWTH of Christ's glorious church share some inspiring parallels. Consider that America's Founders gathered at Independence Hall on July 4, 1776, to establish a nation that would be a beacon of hope and freedom to countless millions throughout the generations. Similarly, Christ's disciples gathered in Jerusalem to establish a church destined to take the hope of the gospel to the ends of the earth. Acts recounts the bold steps of faith the apostles took after they were filled with the power of the Holy Spirit. God used them to establish an ever-growing community of believers that models Christian virtue and faith in this dark, sin-filled world.

Just as America's Founding Fathers did, those early Christians faced many challenges, real dangers, and much opposition. But by God's grace as well as with prayer, hard work, and a steadfast reliance on the Almighty, they took the truth of the gospel to Jerusalem, Judea, Samaria, and the ends of the earth. Even today, the gospel of Jesus is the only hope for peace upon which individuals—or nations—can rely.

*"You are My witnesses," says the LORD,*
*"And My servant whom I have chosen,*
*That you may know and believe Me,*
*And understand that I am He.*
*Before Me there was no God formed,*
*Nor shall there be after Me.*
*I, even I, am the LORD,*
*And besides Me there is no savior."*

ISAIAH 43:10–11

*But you shall receive power when the Holy Spirit has come upon you; and you shall be witnesses to Me in Jerusalem, and in all Judea and Samaria, and to the end of the earth.*

ACTS 1:8

*If anyone thirsts, let him come to Me and drink. He who believes in Me, as the Scripture has said, out of his heart will flow rivers of living water.*

JOHN 7:37–38

# Would You Die?

ACCORDING TO POPULAR LEGEND, JOHN HANCOCK SIGNED his name largely and distinctly to the Declaration of Independence so King George could read it without spectacles. While that may not be true, it is true that Mr. Hancock put his life on the line with that signature.

Each of the fifty-six signers knew the risk: "With a firm reliance on the protection of divine Providence, we mutually pledge to each other our Lives, our Fortunes, and our sacred Honor."[88]

The year before signing the Declaration, Patrick Henry addressed the Virginia Convention:

> We are not weak if we make a proper use of those means which the God of nature hath placed in our power. . . . Besides, sir, we shall not fight our battles alone. There is a just God who presides over the destinies of nations, and who will raise up friends to fight our battles for us.[89]

Yet in the early 1990s the authors of *The Day America Told the Truth* polled Americans about which beliefs they would die for—48 percent said "none." Only 30 percent would die for God, and fewer would die for their country.[90]

*This is My commandment, that you love one another as I have loved you. Greater love has no one than this, than to lay down one's life for his friends.*

JOHN 15:12–13

*For to me, to live is Christ, and to die is gain. But if I live on in the flesh, this will mean fruit from my labor; yet what I shall choose I cannot tell.*

PHILIPPIANS 1:21–22

*I beseech you therefore, brethren, by the mercies of God, that you present your bodies a living sacrifice, holy, acceptable to God, which is your reasonable service. And do not be conformed to this world, but be transformed by the renewing of your mind, that you may prove what is that good and acceptable and perfect will of God.*

ROMANS 12:1–2

# Revival in America

WHEN JONATHAN EDWARDS BEGAN PREACHING IN THE town of Northampton, Massachusetts, in 1734, the moral conditions of that colony and throughout the British settlements were at an extreme low. The New England that was to be a "city on the hill" had become materialistic, the strict Puritan teachings no longer followed.

From the pulpit, Edwards stressed the importance of an immediate, personal spiritual rebirth. He preached the unworthiness of sinful man and the grace of God upon which any of us is totally dependent for salvation—and a revival began in his church, first among the youth and then spreading to the adults.

Edwards wrote that "in the spring and summer following, A.D. 1735, the town seemed to be so full of the presence of God. It never was so full of love, nor of joy, and yet so full of distress, as it was then."[91] In two years, three hundred converts were added to the church, and news of the revival spread throughout New England.

*For God so loved the world that He gave His only begotten Son, that whoever believes in Him should not perish but have everlasting life. For God did not send His Son into the world to condemn the world, but that the world through Him might be saved.*

JOHN 3:16–17

*That if you confess with your mouth the Lord Jesus and believe in your heart that God has raised Him from the dead, you will be saved. For with the heart one believes unto righteousness, and with the mouth confession is made unto salvation.*

ROMANS 10:9–10

*For by grace you have been saved through faith, and that not of yourselves; it is the gift of God.*

EPHESIANS 2:8

# A War Hero Without a Gun

MEDIC DESMOND DOSS ENTERED THE US ARMY IN APRIL 1942 AS a conscientious objector because of his religious beliefs. From the beginning, men in his company harassed Doss for his faith.

On Okinawa, in late spring of 1945, his battalion assaulted a jagged escarpment four hundred feet high—only to be met with artillery, mortar, and machine-gun fire that inflicted approximately seventy-five casualties. Doss remained with the many stricken, carrying them one by one to the edge of the cliff and lowering them down its face. Each time he prayed, "Dear God, let me get just one more man."[92]

In three more battles in May, Doss unhesitatingly braved enemy artillery, mortar shells, and grenades to dress his fellow soldiers' wounds and evacuate them to safety. On May 21, he was seriously wounded when a grenade exploded. He waited five hours before litter bearers reached him.

Discovering he had lost his Bible, Doss asked the men to watch for it. Every able man combed the battlefield until one found the Bible and mailed it to Doss.

Private First Class Doss became the first conscientious objector during World War II to receive the Medal of Honor for bravery.[93]

*The wicked flee when no one pursues,*
*But the righteous are bold as a lion.*

PROVERBS 28:1

*Praying always with all prayer and supplication in the Spirit, being watchful to this end with all perseverance and supplication for all the saints—and for me, that utterance may be given to me, that I may open my mouth boldly to make known the mystery of the gospel.*

EPHESIANS 6:18–19

*Let your conduct be without covetousness; be content with such things as you have. For He Himself has said, "I will never leave you nor forsake you." So we may boldly say:*

*"The Lord is my helper;*
*I will not fear.*
*What can man do to me?"*

HEBREWS 13:5–6

# Son of Man and Son of God

WITH THE COMPASSION OF A FAMILY PHYSICIAN, DR. LUKE penned the gospel that bears his name, carefully documenting the perfect humanity of Jesus Christ. Luke built this gospel narrative on the foundation of historical reliability, emphasizing Jesus' ancestry, birth, and early life before moving chronologically through His earthly ministry. Growing belief and growing opposition develop side by side, with the opposition finally sending the Son of Man to His death on the cross. But Jesus' resurrection ensured that His purpose of saving the lost was fulfilled.

Christianity welcomes close examination, that the inquirer might "know the certainty" of its truths (Luke 1:4). Alexander Hamilton, a signer of the Constitution and one of America's first constitutional lawyers, made such an investigation. This is his conclusion: "I have examined carefully the evidence of the Christian religion; and, if I was sitting as a juror upon its authenticity, I would unhesitatingly give my verdict in its favor. . . . I can prove its truth as clearly as any proposition ever submitted to the mind of man."[94]

*Then Jesus said to them, "When you lift up the Son of Man, then you will know that I am He, and that I do nothing of Myself; but as My Father taught Me, I speak these things. And He who sent Me is with Me. The Father has not left Me alone, for I always do those things that please Him."*

JOHN 8:28–29

*Most assuredly, I say to you, the hour is coming, and now is, when the dead will hear the voice of the Son of God; and those who hear will live. For as the Father has life in Himself, so He has granted the Son to have life in Himself.*

JOHN 5:25–26

*For the Son of Man has come to seek and to save that which was lost.*

LUKE 19:10

# Serving in the Church

PAUL, THE AGED AND EXPERIENCED APOSTLE, WROTE TO THE young pastor Timothy, who was facing a heavy burden of responsibility in the church at Ephesus. False teachings needed to be corrected; public worship, safeguarded; and mature leadership, developed. Paul spoke pointedly about a minister's proper conduct and counseled Timothy on the qualities that make for a godly leader. A Christ follower must be careful to avoid false teachers and greedy motives, pursuing instead righteousness, godliness, faith, love, perseverance, and the gentleness that befit a servant of God.

As he took over responsibility for the church Paul founded at Ephesus, Timothy could not be a second Paul, but he would need to use all his God-given strengths to lead the church. Likewise, American writer and humorist Charles F. Browne said, "We can't all be Washingtons, but we can all be patriots."[95] We will never be the father of our country, but we can serve our country to the best of our abilities.

*For you, brethren, have been called to liberty; only do not use liberty as an opportunity for the flesh, but through love serve one another.*

GALATIANS 5:13

*For if the blood of bulls and goats and the ashes of a heifer, sprinkling the unclean, sanctifies for the purifying of the flesh, how much more shall the blood of Christ, who through the eternal Spirit offered Himself without spot to God, cleanse your conscience from dead works to serve the living God?*

HEBREWS 9:13–14

*Serve the* L*ORD with gladness;*
*Come before His presence with singing.*
*Know that the* L*ORD, He is God;*
*It is He who has made us, and not we ourselves;*
*We are His people and the sheep of His pasture.*

PSALM 100:2–3

# The Bible's Influence

IN 1984, UNIVERSITY OF HOUSTON POLITICAL SCIENTISTS Donald Lutz and Charles Hyneman wrote about the sources that most influenced the development of American political thought during our nation's founding era, from 1760 to 1805.[96]

After analyzing some fifteen thousand items published during that forty-five-year period, the authors isolated 3,154 direct quotes cited by the Founders and discovered that 34 percent came directly out of the Bible. French legal philosopher Baron Charles de Montesquieu was quoted 8.3 percent of the time. Sir William Blackstone, a renowned English jurist whose *Commentaries on the Laws of England* were highly accepted in America, was next at 7.9 percent, and English philosopher John Locke was fourth with 2.9 percent.

Three-fourths of the biblical citations came from reprinted sermons, and only 9 percent came from secular literature. These statistics clearly reflect the Bible's impact on the Founding Fathers.

*As for God, His way is perfect;*
*The word of the LORD is proven;*
*He is a shield to all who trust in Him.*
*For who is God, except the LORD?*
*And who is a rock, except our God?*

PSALM 18:30–31

*For the word of God is living and powerful, and sharper than any two-edged sword, piercing even to the division of soul and spirit, and of joints and marrow, and is a discerner of the thoughts and intents of the heart.*

HEBREWS 4:12

*So shall My word be that goes forth from My mouth;*
*It shall not return to Me void,*
*But it shall accomplish what I please,*
*And it shall prosper in the thing for which I sent it.*

ISAIAH 55:11

# The Cornerstone of American Society

RONALD REAGAN, THE FORTIETH PRESIDENT OF THE UNITED States (1981–1989), wrote the following:

> The family has always been the cornerstone of American society. Our families nurture, preserve and pass on to each succeeding generation the values we share and cherish, values that are the foundation for our freedoms. In the family, we learn our first lessons of God and man, love and discipline, rights and responsibilities, human dignity and human frailty.
>
> Our families give us daily examples of these lessons being put into practice. In raising and instructing our children; in providing personal and compassionate care for the elderly; in bringing the handicapped into the mainstream of community life; in maintaining the spiritual strength of religious commitment among our people—in these and other ways, America's families make immeasurable contributions to America's well-being.
>
> Today more than ever, it is essential that these contributions not be taken for granted and that each of us remember that the strength of our families is vital to the strength of our Nation.[97]

*God sets the solitary in families;*
*He brings out those who are bound into prosperity.*

PSALM 68:6

*Honor your father and your mother, that your days may be long upon the land which the* Lord *your God is giving you.*

EXODUS 20:12

*Now, therefore, you are no longer strangers and foreigners, but fellow citizens with the saints and members of the household of God, having been built on the foundation of the apostles and prophets, Jesus Christ Himself being the chief cornerstone, in whom the whole building, being fitted together, grows into a holy temple in the Lord, in whom you also are being built together for a dwelling place of God in the Spirit.*

EPHESIANS 2:19–22

# The Power of God

AS THE PRESIDENT OF YALE COLLEGE, EZRA STILES SPOKE before the governor and the General Assembly of Connecticut in May 1783:

> In our lowest and most dangerous state . . . we sustained ourselves against the British Army of sixty thousand troops, commanded by . . . the ablest generals Britain could procure . . . with a naval force of 22,000 seamen. . . .
>
> Who but a Washington, inspired by heaven, could have struck out the movement and maneuver of Princeton? To whom but the ruler of the winds shall we ascribe it, that the British reinforcement . . . was delayed on the ocean three months by contrary winds?
>
> What but a providential miracle detected the conspiracy of *Arnold* . . . in which the body of the American army . . . were to have been rendered into the hands of the enemy! . . .
>
> It is God who so ordered the balancing interests of nations. . . .
>
> The United States are under peculiar obligations to become a holy people unto the Lord our God.[98]

*God has spoken once,*
*Twice I have heard this:*
*That power belongs to God.*
*Also to You, O Lord, belongs mercy;*
*For You render to each one according to his work.*

PSALM 62:11–12

*For the Scripture says to the Pharaoh, "For this very purpose I have raised you up, that I may show My power in you, and that My name may be declared in all the earth." Therefore He has mercy on whom He wills, and whom He wills He hardens.*

ROMANS 9:17–18

*For the message of the cross is foolishness to those who are perishing, but to us who are being saved it is the power of God.*

I CORINTHIANS 1:18

# "Duty, Honor, Country"

IN HIS MAY 12, 1962, FAREWELL SPEECH TO THE CORPS OF Cadets at West Point, General Douglas MacArthur gave a moving tribute to the American soldier. The following paragraph is from that stirring speech:

> Duty, Honor, Country. . . .
>
> The code which those words perpetuate embraces the highest moral laws and will stand the test of any ethics or philosophies ever promulgated for the uplift of mankind. Its requirements are for the things that are right, and its restraints are from the things that are wrong. The soldier, above all other men, is required to practice the greatest act of religious training—sacrifice. In battle and in the face of danger and death, he discloses those divine attributes which his Maker gave when He created man in His own image. No physical courage and no brute instinct can take the place of the Divine help which alone can sustain [the soldier]. However horrible the incidents of war may be, the soldier who is called upon to offer and to give his life for his country is the noblest development of mankind.[99]

*The* Lord *is my rock and my fortress and my*
*deliverer;*
*My God, my strength, in whom I will trust;*
*My shield and the horn of my salvation, my*
*stronghold.*

PSALM 18:2

*Honor and majesty are before Him;*
*Strength and beauty are in His sanctuary.*
*Give to the* Lord*, O families of the peoples,*
*Give to the* Lord *glory and strength.*
*Give to the* Lord *the glory due His name.*

PSALM 96:6–8

*For this is the will of God, that by doing good you may put to silence the ignorance of foolish men—as free, yet not using liberty as a cloak for vice, but as bondservants of God. Honor all people. Love the brotherhood. Fear God. Honor the king.*

I PETER 2:15–17

# The Jewish State, 1948

ACCORDING TO MARGARET TRUMAN, THE MOST DIFFICULT decision Harry S. Truman faced as president was whether to support the creation of a Jewish homeland in Palestine after World War II. "I am trying to . . . make the whole world safe for Jews," he wrote.[100] In November 1947, he lobbied for the United Nations' resolution that divided Palestine into Jewish and Arab states.

Great Britain announced it would transfer its authority over Palestine to the United Nations by May 14, 1948. On the eve of British withdrawal, most American experts strongly opposed the creation of a Jewish state, warning Truman that Arab countries would cut off oil and unite to destroy the Jews. But Truman weighed the multifaceted concerns and held firm.

The nation's first prime minister, David Ben-Gurion, read a declaration of Jewish independence: "The name of our state shall be Israel."[101] At midnight, British rule over Palestine lapsed; eleven minutes later, White House spokesman Charlie Ross announced US recognition. The American statement recognizing the new State of Israel bears President Truman's last-minute handwritten changes.

With Truman's decision, the hopes of the Jewish people were realized.

*The Lord builds up Jerusalem;*
*He gathers together the outcasts of Israel.*
*He heals the brokenhearted*
*And binds up their wounds.*

PSALM 147:2–3

*If I forget you, O Jerusalem,*
*Let my right hand forget its skill!*
*If I do not remember you,*
*Let my tongue cling to the roof of my mouth—*
*If I do not exalt Jerusalem*
*Above my chief joy.*

PSALM 137:5–6

*Pray for the peace of Jerusalem:*
*"May they prosper who love you.*
*Peace be within your walls,*
*Prosperity within your palaces."*
*For the sake of my brethren and companions,*
*I will now say, "Peace be within you."*

PSALM 122:6–8

# Genuinely Good Works

FOUNDING FATHER BENJAMIN FRANKLIN WROTE THE FOLlowing:

> I can only show my gratitude for these mercies from God, by a readiness to help his other children and my brethren. For I do not think that thanks and compliments tho' repeated weekly, can discharge our real obligations to each other, and much less those to our Creator. . . .
>
> The faith you mention has certainly its use in the world. . . . But I wish it were more productive of good works than I have generally seen it. I mean real good works, works of kindness, charity, mercy, and public spirit; not holiday-keeping, sermon reading or hearing, performing church ceremonies, or making long prayers, filled with flatteries and compliments. . . .
>
> The worship of God is a duty; the hearing and reading of sermons may be useful; but, if men rest in hearing and praying, as too many do, it is as if a tree should value itself on being water'd and putting forth leaves, tho' it never produc'd any fruit.[102]

*For we are His workmanship, created in Christ Jesus for good works, which God prepared beforehand that we should walk in them.*

EPHESIANS 2:10

*But in a great house there are not only vessels of gold and silver, but also of wood and clay, some for honor and some for dishonor. Therefore if anyone cleanses himself from the latter, he will be a vessel for honor, sanctified and useful for the Master, prepared for every good work.*

2 TIMOTHY 2:20–21

*Either make the tree good and its fruit good, or else make the tree bad and its fruit bad; for a tree is known by its fruit. . . . A good man out of the good treasure of his heart brings forth good things, and an evil man out of the evil treasure brings forth evil things. . . . For by your words you will be justified, and by your words you will be condemned.*

MATTHEW 12:33, 35, 37

# God's Bigger Shovel

FRUSTRATED AT HIS FIRST JOB—MOVING DIRT BY HAND—R. G. LeTourneau (1888–1969) was committed to finding a better, more efficient way to get the work done. As the father of the modern earthmoving industry, he is credited with nearly three hundred inventions, including the bulldozer, scrapers of all sorts, dredgers, portable cranes, and many others. During World War II, he produced 70 percent of all the US Army's earthmoving machinery.[103]

With Matthew 6:33 as his life verse, LeTourneau felt called to be a "businessman for God," saying that God was the Chairman of his board. He established the LeTourneau Foundation to channel 90 percent of his multimillion-dollar salary to Christian endeavors. LeTourneau was convinced that he could not outgive God. In his autobiography, he remembered something one of his customers shared with him: "I try to shovel out more for God than He can for me, but He always wins. He's got a bigger shovel."[104]

LeTourneau's business efforts never deterred him from his reason for existence: to glorify God and spread the gospel. He shared his faith with millions, founded missionary efforts in Liberia and Peru, and, with his wife, founded LeTourneau University in Longview, Texas, which has produced more than twenty-five thousand alumni who are serving the Lord worldwide.

*For he who sows to his flesh will of the flesh reap corruption, but he who sows to the Spirit will of the Spirit reap everlasting life. And let us not grow weary while doing good, for in due season we shall reap if we do not lose heart.*

GALATIANS 6:8–9

*But seek first the kingdom of God and His righteousness, and all these things shall be added to you. Therefore do not worry about tomorrow, for tomorrow will worry about its own things. Sufficient for the day is its own trouble.*

MATTHEW 6:33–34

*Give, and it will be given to you: good measure, pressed down, shaken together, and running over will be put into your bosom. For with the same measure that you use, it will be measured back to you.*

LUKE 6:38

# Lighting the World

A PHILANTHROPIST LATER IN LIFE, SAMUEL COLGATE (1822–1897) was the American manufacturer whose industriousness resulted in the Colgate-Palmolive Company. Clearly he recognized Jesus as God's Son and the value of the Word:

> The only spiritual light in the world comes through Jesus Christ and the inspired Book; redemption and forgiveness of sin alone through Christ. Without His presence and the teachings of the Bible, we would be enshrouded in moral darkness and despair.
>
> The condition of those nations without a Christ, contrasted with those where Christ is accepted, reveals so marked a difference that no arguments are needed. It is an object-lesson so plain that it can be seen and understood by all. May "the earth be full of the knowledge of the Lord, as the waters cover the sea."[105]

*Nor do they light a lamp and put it under a basket, but on a lampstand, and it gives light to all who are in the house. Let your light so shine before men, that they may see your good works and glorify your Father in heaven.*

MATTHEW 5:15–16

*Then Jesus said to them, "A little while longer the light is with you. Walk while you have the light, lest darkness overtake you; he who walks in darkness does not know where he is going. While you have the light, believe in the light, that you may become sons of light."*

JOHN 12:35–36

*For you were once darkness, but now you are light in the Lord. Walk as children of light (for the fruit of the Spirit is in all goodness, righteousness, and truth), finding out what is acceptable to the Lord.*

EPHESIANS 5:8–10

# A Day of Fasting

AFTER THE BOSTON TEA PARTY, THE BRITISH NAVY RETALIATED by blockading the port of Boston. The colonies surrounding Massachusetts responded with sympathy and action. On May 24, 1774, the House of Burgesses in Virginia proposed and approved a Day of Fasting, Humiliation, and Prayer:

> This House being deeply impressed with Apprehension of the great Dangers to be derived to British America from the hostile Invasion of the City of Boston . . . whose Commerce and Harbour are on the 1st Day of June next to be stopped by an armed Force, deem it highly necessary that the said first Day of June be set apart . . . as a Day of Fasting, Humiliation, and Prayer, devoutly to implore the divine Interposition for averting the heavy Calamity, which threatens Destruction to our civil Rights, and the Evils of civil War; to give us one Heart and one Mind firmly to oppose . . . every Injury to American Rights, and that the Minds of his Majesty and his Parliament may be inspired from above with Wisdom, Moderation, and Justice, to remove from the loyal People of America all Cause of Danger from a continued Pursuit of Measures pregnant with their Ruin.[106]

*"Now, therefore," says the LORD,*
*"Turn to Me with all your heart,*
*With fasting, with weeping, and with mourning."*
*So rend your heart, and not your garments;*
*Return to the LORD your God,*
*For He is gracious and merciful,*
*Slow to anger, and of great kindness;*
*And He relents from doing harm.*

JOEL 2:12–13

*Assuredly, I say to you, if you have faith as a mustard seed, you will say to this mountain, "Move from here to there," and it will move; and nothing will be impossible for you. However, this kind does not go out except by prayer and fasting.*

MATTHEW 17:20–21

*But you, when you fast, anoint your head and wash your face, so that you do not appear to men to be fasting, but to your Father who is in the secret place; and your Father who sees in secret will reward you openly.*

MATTHEW 6:17–18

# God's Laws for God's Creatures

THE DECLARATION OF INDEPENDENCE DECLARED NOT ONLY the colonies' independence from Britain, but also a dependence on "the Laws of Nature and of Nature's God." These had been defined by historic legal writers, such as Sir William Blackstone, as the laws that God had established for the governance of people, nations, and nature. Blackstone's *Commentaries on the Law*, the primary law book of the Founding Fathers, defined "the laws of nature" as the will of God for man.

> Man, considered as a creature, must necessarily be subject to the laws of his creator, for he is entirely a dependent being. . . . It is necessary that he should in all points conform to his maker's will. This will of his maker is called the law of nature. . . . It is binding over all the globe, in all countries, and at all times: no human laws are of any validity, if contrary to this. . . .
>
> But every man now finds . . . that his reason is corrupt, and his understanding full of ignorance and error. . . . The doctrines thus delivered we call the revealed or divine law, and they are to be found only in the holy scriptures. . . .
>
> Upon these two foundations . . . no human laws should be suffered to contradict these.[107]

*Only may the* L*ORD* *give you wisdom and understanding, and give you charge concerning Israel, that you may keep the law of the* L*ORD* *your God. Then you will prosper, if you take care to fulfill the statutes and judgments with which the* L*ORD* *charged Moses concerning Israel. Be strong and of good courage; do not fear nor be dismayed.*

I CHRONICLES 22:12–13

*Blessed is the man*
*Who walks not in the counsel of the ungodly,*
*Nor stands in the path of sinners,*
*Nor sits in the seat of the scornful;*
*But his delight is in the law of the* L*ORD*,
*And in His law he meditates day and night.*

PSALM 1:1–2

*Blessed are the undefiled in the way,*
*Who walk in the law of the* L*ORD*!
*Blessed are those who keep His testimonies,*
*Who seek Him with the whole heart!*

PSALM 119:1–2

# Sunday School

NOTICING THE MIGRATION WEST FROM THE APPALACHIAN cabins to settlements along the Oregon Trail, the American Sunday School Union (ASSU) set as a goal to establish a Sunday school in every new community on the Western frontier and sent out a large number of missionaries to make that happen. These Sunday schools eventually gave rise to thousands of churches across America.

One example of the tremendous influence the Sunday school movement had in American frontier life was the Mississippi Valley Enterprise (MVE), the effort of the ASSU to "establish a Sunday-school in every destitute place where it is practicable, throughout the Valley of the Mississippi."[108] In fifty years, the MVE established over 61,000 Sunday schools and enrolled 2,650,000 pupils.[109] Remarkably, during his twenty years of service, missionary Stephen Paxson, who was born with a speech impediment that later earned him the nickname "Stuttering Stephen," started 1,314 Sunday schools that taught 83,000 students about Jesus' love for them.[110]

*So then faith comes by hearing, and hearing by the word of God.*

ROMANS 10:17

*Listen carefully to Me, and eat what is good,*
*And let your soul delight itself in abundance.*
*Incline your ear, and come to Me.*
*Hear, and your soul shall live.*

ISAIAH 55:2–3

*And you shall teach them the statutes and the laws, and show them the way in which they must walk and the work they must do.*

EXODUS 18:20

*Teach me Your way, O LORD,*
*And lead me in a smooth path.*

PSALM 27:11

# Wisdom and Instruction for Life

THERE IS NO BETTER SOURCE OF PRACTICAL WISDOM AND instruction for how to live an upright and righteous life than the book of Proverbs. Its counsel, however, is not just relevant to individuals, but to nations as well. Proverbs 14:34, for instance, is a truth that godly leaders have cited for generations: "Righteousness exalts a nation, but sin is a reproach to any people."

Patrick Henry, one of early America's most outspoken Revolutionary leaders, predicted that whether or not the newly formed United States would prove "a blessing or a curse, will depend upon the use our people make of the blessings which a gracious God hath bestowed on us. If they are wise, they will be great and happy. If they are of a contrary character, they will be miserable. Righteousness alone can exalt them as a nation."[111]

The state of our nation today suggests we have strayed from God's wisdom. We—as individuals and corporately as a nation—must seek God and His righteousness if we are to continue in His grace.

*Get wisdom! Get understanding!*
*Do not forget, nor turn away from the words of my mouth.*
*Do not forsake her, and she will preserve you;*
*Love her, and she will keep you.*
*Wisdom is the principal thing;*
*Therefore get wisdom.*
*And in all your getting, get understanding.*

PROVERBS 4:5–7

*He who heeds the word wisely will find good,*
*And whoever trusts in the LORD, happy is he.*
*The wise in heart will be called prudent,*
*And sweetness of the lips increases learning.*

PROVERBS 16:20–21

# God's Providence

ON MEMORIAL DAY IN 1923, CALVIN COOLIDGE, THE THIRTIETH president of the United States, spoke about the Puritan forefathers:

> If there be a destiny, it is of no avail for us unless we work with it. The ways of Providence will be of no advantage to us unless we proceed in the same direction. If we perceive a destiny in America, if we believe that Providence has been our guide, our own success, our own salvation requires that we should act and serve in harmony and obedience. . . .
>
> Settlers came here from mixed motives, some for pillage and adventure, some for trade and refuge, but those who have set their imperishable mark upon our institutions came from far higher motives. . . . They were intent upon establishing a Christian commonwealth in accordance with the principle of self-government.
>
> They were an inspired body of men. . . . They had a genius for organized society on the foundation of piety, righteousness, liberty, and obedience to law. They brought with them the accumulated wisdom and experience of the ages. . . . Who can fail to see . . . the hand of destiny? Who can doubt that it has been guided by a Divine Providence?[112]

*Therefore be careful to observe them; for this is your wisdom and your understanding in the sight of the peoples who will hear all these statutes, and say, "Surely this great nation is a wise and understanding people."*

DEUTERONOMY 4:6

*Bondservants, be obedient to those who are your masters according to the flesh, with fear and trembling, in sincerity of heart, as to Christ; not with eye service, as men-pleasers, but as bondservants of Christ, doing the will of God from the heart, with goodwill doing service, as to the Lord, and not to men, knowing that whatever good anyone does, he will receive the same from the Lord, whether he is a slave or free.*

EPHESIANS 6:5–8

# Circuit Riders and Farmer-Preachers

AS AMERICANS MOVED WEST IN THE LATE 1700S, PREACHERS braved cold weather, lack of roads, and threat of attacks to take the gospel to the pioneers.

Led by the colossal efforts of Francis Asbury, who traveled nearly 300,000 miles on horseback and preached more than 16,000 sermons, an army of Methodist circuit riders was inspired to go wherever the pioneers went.[113] In that span of time, the denomination grew in number from only 300 members with four ministers to over 200,000 members with 2,000 ministers, many of whom had little formal education.[114] The Methodists also gave unprecedented freedom to both women and Black Americans.

Similarly, the Baptists sent out "farmer-preachers." Most of them had little education and were poorly paid, but they were in touch with the pioneers' lives. With an emphasis on the need for a personal conversion and salvation from sin through faith in Jesus Christ, these ministers spread the gospel far and wide. The Baptists made it easy for committed laypeople to be involved in God's kingdom work.

*And He said to them, "Go into all the world and preach the gospel to every creature. He who believes and is baptized will be saved."*

MARK 16:15–16

*The Spirit of the* LORD *is upon Me,*
*Because He has anointed Me*
*To preach the gospel to the poor;*
*He has sent Me to heal the brokenhearted,*
*To proclaim liberty to the captives*
*And recovery of sight to the blind,*
*To set at liberty those who are oppressed;*
*To proclaim the acceptable year of the* LORD.

LUKE 4:18–19

*I charge you therefore before God and the Lord Jesus Christ, who will judge the living and the dead at His appearing and His kingdom: Preach the word! Be ready in season and out of season. Convince, rebuke, exhort, with all longsuffering and teaching.*

2 TIMOTHY 4:1–2

# Words for a College Graduate

WILLIAM SAMUEL JOHNSON (1727–1819), PRESIDENT OF Columbia University (King's College before 1784), spoke to one of the first graduating classes after the Revolutionary War:

> You have . . . received a public education, the purpose whereof hath been to qualify you the better to serve your Creator and your country. . . . Your first great duties . . . are those you owe to Heaven, to your Creator and Redeemer. Let these be ever present to your minds, and exemplified in your lives and conduct. . . .
>
> The fear of God is the beginning of wisdom, and its consummation is everlasting felicity. . . . Remember, too, that you are the redeemed of the Lord, that you are bought with a price, even the inestimable price of the precious blood of the Son of God. Adore Jehovah, therefore, as your God and your Judge. Love, fear, and serve Him as your Creator, Redeemer, and Sanctifier. . . .
>
> Make Him your friend and protector and your felicity is secured both here and hereafter.[115]

*And now, Israel, what does the* Lord *your God require of you, but to fear the* Lord *your God, to walk in all His ways and to love Him, to serve the* Lord *your God with all your heart and with all your soul, and to keep the commandments of the* Lord *and His statutes which I command you today for your good?*

DEUTERONOMY 10:12–13

*Trust in the* Lord *with all your heart,*
*And lean not on your own understanding;*
*In all your ways acknowledge Him,*
*And He shall direct your paths.*

PROVERBS 3:5–6

*Take My yoke upon you and learn from Me, for I am gentle and lowly in heart, and you will find rest for your souls. For My yoke is easy and My burden is light.*

MATTHEW 11:29–30

# The Key to Survival

ON JUNE 2, 1995, US AIR FORCE CAPTAIN SCOTT O'GRADY WAS patrolling the United Nations designated no-fly zone over war-torn Bosnia when, at 27,000 feet, his F-16 fighter was struck by a surface-to-air missile. He desperately pulled his ejection lever and was catapulted into the sky at 350 miles per hour. Remarkably, he managed to land unscathed—but in enemy territory.

For six incredible days and nights, O'Grady eluded capture by the Bosnian Serbs who relentlessly pursued him. Relying in part on his military survival training, O'Grady said his faith in God also sustained him. During his third day on the ground, he experienced the love of God to such a degree that it took away his fear of death. On the sixth day, in a daring daylight rescue, an elite team of Marines moved in with a chopper, dodged enemy fire, and pulled the young American to safety.[116]

At a national press conference following his triumphant return to the United States, O'Grady said, "If it wasn't for God's love for me and my love for God, I wouldn't have gotten through it."[117]

*Wait on the* L*ORD;*
*Be of good courage,*
*And He shall strengthen your heart;*
*Wait, I say, on the* L*ORD!*

PSALM 27:14

*The* L*ORD is my light and my salvation;*
*Whom shall I fear?*
*The* L*ORD is the strength of my life;*
*Of whom shall I be afraid?*

PSALM 27:1

*He who dwells in the secret place of the Most High*
*Shall abide under the shadow of the Almighty.*
*I will say of the* L*ORD, "He is my refuge and my fortress;*
*My God, in Him I will trust."*

PSALM 91:1–2

# God's Light

IN JUNE 1630, JOHN WINTHROP LANDED IN MASSACHUSETTS Bay with seven hundred people in eleven ships, thus beginning the Great Migration. During this sixteen-year period, more than twenty thousand Puritans sailed for New England. The Puritans so believed that this New World would be free of the corruptions in their own church-state homeland, they called their colony a "Zion in the wilderness"[118] and "a city upon a hill."[119] Winthrop stated that the aim of the colonists was "to advance the kingdom of our Lord Jesus Christ, and to enjoy the liberties of the gospel in purity with peace."[120]

In 1638, the Reverend John Davenport and Theophilus Eaton established a colony in New Haven, Connecticut. A year later, the Fundamental Orders of Connecticut was adopted.

> For as much as it hath pleased Almighty God by the wise disposition of his divine providence . . . and well knowing where a people are gathered together the word of God requires that to maintain the peace and union of such a people there should be an orderly and decent Government established according to God, to order and dispose of the affairs of the people at all seasons as occasion shall require.[121]

*You are the light of the world. A city that is set on a hill cannot be hidden. Nor do they light a lamp and put it under a basket, but on a lampstand, and it gives light to all who are in the house. Let your light so shine before men, that they may see your good works and glorify your Father in heaven.*

MATTHEW 5:14–16

*Then Jesus spoke to them again, saying, "I am the light of the world. He who follows Me shall not walk in darkness, but have the light of life."*

JOHN 8:12

*This is the message which we have heard from Him and declare to you, that God is light and in Him is no darkness at all. If we say that we have fellowship with Him, and walk in darkness, we lie and do not practice the truth. But if we walk in the light as He is in the light, we have fellowship with one another, and the blood of Jesus Christ His Son cleanses us from all sin.*

I JOHN 1:5–7

# A D-Day Prayer

PRESIDENT FRANKLIN D. ROOSEVELT READ THIS PRAYER, ORIGInally titled "Let Our Hearts Be Stout," over radio to an anxious nation as Allied troops were invading Nazi-occupied Europe on D-Day, June 6, 1944:

> Almighty God: Our sons, pride of our Nation, this day have set upon a mighty endeavor, a struggle to preserve our Republic, our religion, and our civilization, and to set free a suffering humanity. Lead them straight and true; give strength to their arms, stoutness to their hearts, steadfastness in their faith.
>
> They will need Thy blessings. Their road will be long and hard. . . .
>
> [Our men] fight to liberate. They fight to let justice arise, and tolerance and good will among all Thy people. They yearn but for the end of battle, for their return to the haven of home. Some will never return. Embrace these, Father, and receive them, Thy heroic servants, into Thy kingdom. . . .
>
> With Thy blessing, we shall prevail over the unholy forces of our enemy. . . .
>
> Thy will be done, Almighty God. Amen.[122]

*O Lord, God of my salvation,*
*I have cried out day and night before You.*
*Let my prayer come before You;*
*Incline Your ear to my cry.*
*For my soul is full of troubles.*

PSALM 88:1–3

*The Lord will command His lovingkindness in the daytime,*
*And in the night His song shall be with me—*
*A prayer to the God of my life.*

PSALM 42:8

*Now therefore, our God, hear the prayer of Your servant, and his supplications, and for the Lord's sake cause Your face to shine on Your sanctuary, which is desolate.*

DANIEL 9:17

# America on Its Knees

FOUNDER OF THE HILTON HOTEL CHAIN, CONRAD HILTON (1887–1979), published this prayer on full-page ads in major magazines on July 4, 1952:

*Our Father in heaven.*

*We pray that You save us from ourselves.*

*The world that You have made for us, to live in peace, we have made into an armed camp. We live in fear of war to come. We are afraid of "the terror that flies by night, and the arrow that flies by day, the pestilence that walks in darkness and the destruction that wastes at noon-day."*

*We have turned from You to go our selfish way. We have broken Your commandments and denied Your truth. We have left Your altars to serve the false gods of money and pleasure and power.*

*Forgive us and help us.*

*Now, darkness gathers around us and we are confused in all our counsels. Losing faith in You, we lose faith in ourselves. . . .*

*Be swift to save us, dear God, before the darkness falls.*[123]

*But You, O Lord, are a shield for me,*
*My glory and the One who lifts up my head.*

PSALM 3:3

*Let us hold fast the confession of our hope without wavering, for He who promised is faithful. And let us consider one another in order to stir up love and good works.*

HEBREWS 10:23–24

*Get wisdom! Get understanding!*
*Do not forget, nor turn away from the words of my mouth.*
*Do not forsake her, and she will preserve you;*
*Love her, and she will keep you.*
*Wisdom is the principal thing;*
*Therefore get wisdom.*
*And in all your getting, get understanding.*

PROVERBS 4:5–7

# Notes

1. Ronald Reagan, "Remarks at the Annual Convention of the National Religious Broadcasters," January 31, 1983, Ronald Reagan Presidential Library & Museum, National Archives, https://www.reaganlibrary.gov/archives/speech/remarks-annual-convention-national-religious-broadcasters-0.
2. George Washington, "Thanksgiving Proclamation, 3 October 1789," Founders Online, National Archives, https://founders.archives.gov/documents/Washington/05-04-02-0091.
3. Declaration of Independence, July 4, 1776, transcript, National Archives, https://www.archives.gov/founding-docs/declaration-transcript.
4. Declaration of Independence.
5. *American Dictionary of the English Language*, "patriotism," accessed November 5, 2025, https://webstersdictionary1828.com/Dictionary/patriotism.
6. *Merriam-Webster Dictionary*, s.v. "patriotism," accessed November 5, 2025, https://www.merriam-webster.com/dictionary/patriotism.
7. Edwin D. Sanborn, *A Eulogy on Daniel Webster, Delivered Before the Students of Phillips Academy, Andover Massachusetts, December 29, 1852* (Dartmouth Press, 1853), 37.
8. Elias Boudinot to Reverend Doctor John B. Romeyn, Burlington, June 5, 1816, in *History of the American Bible Society* by W. P. Strickland (Harper & Brothers, 1850), 353.
9. George Washington Carver to James T. Hardwick, 1928, in *Carver of Tuskegee* by Ethel Edwards (pub. by author, 1971), 157–60.
10. Franklin D. Roosevelt, "Annual Message to Congress," January 4, 1939, The American Presidency Project, UC Santa Barbara, https://www.presidency.ucsb.edu/documents/annual-message-congress.
11. "Obituary: Ruth Bell Graham Dies," Ruth Bell Graham, Billy Graham Evangelistic Association, June 14, 2007, https://ruthbellgrahammemorial.org/obituary/.

12. Ruth Bell Graham, *Prodigals and Those Who Love Them: Words of Encouragement for Those Who Wait* (Baker, 1999), 102.
13. Alexander Hamilton, "The Farmer Refuted, &c., [23 February] 1775," Founders Online, National Archives, https://founders.archives.gov/documents/Hamilton/01-01-02-0057.
14. "Texts of Gov. Stevenson's Speeches Before Legion and Jersey Democrats," *New York Times*, August 28, 1952, https://timesmachine.nytimes.com/timesmachine/1952/08/28/issue.html.
15. "Inaugural Address of George Bush," January 20, 1989, The Avalon Project, Yale Law School, https://avalon.law.yale.edu/20th_century/bush.asp.
16. Henry Wadsworth Longfellow, "The Building of the Ship," Poetry Foundation, accessed November 4, 2025, https://www.poetryfoundation.org/poems/44626/the-building-of-the-ship.
17. "President Franklin D. Roosevelt to Winston Churchill, January 20, 1941," The Library of Congress, https://www.loc.gov/exhibits/churchill/interactive/_html/wc0112.html.
18. "Give Us the Tools, 1941," speech by Winston Churchill, recorded February 9, 1941, America's National Churchill Museum, Westminster College, audio and transcript, https://www.nationalchurchillmuseum.org/give-us-the-tools.html.
19. "Governor Ronald Reagan Speech to the Conservative Political Action Conference (CPAC) in Washington, DC," recorded January 25, 1974, National Archives Catalog, https://catalog.archives.gov/id/169489077.
20. Harry Truman, "Address in Columbus at a Conference of the Federal Council of Churches," March 6, 1946, Harry S. Truman Library & Museum, National Archives, https://www.trumanlibrary.gov/library/public-papers/52/address-columbus-conference-federal-council-churches.
21. Conn. Const. of 1818, pmbl., Office of the Secretary of the State, Connecticut, https://portal.ct.gov/SOTS/Register-Manual/Section-I/1818-Constitution-of-the-State-of-Connecticut.
22. Maine Const. of 1820, pmbl., Maine State Legislature, https://legislature.maine.gov/uploads/originals/const1820.pdf.
23. Mass. Const. of 1780, pmbl., National Constitution Center,

https://constitutioncenter.org/the-constitution/historic-document-library/detail/massachusetts-constitution.

24. "The Story of the Four Chaplains," Virginia War Memorial Foundation, accessed November 4, 2025, https://vawarmemorial.org/the-story-of-the-four-chaplains/.
25. John Quincy Adams to the officers of the literary society in Baltimore, June 22, 1838, in *The American Quarterly Register*, comp. B. B. Edwards and W. Cogswell, vol. 12 (American Education Society, 1840), 86.
26. "Reply to Loyal Colored People of Baltimore upon Presentation of a Bible," in *Collected Works of Abraham Lincoln*, vol. 7 (Rutgers University Press, 1953), University of Michigan Library Digital Collections.
27. Franklin D. Roosevelt, "Statement on the Four Hundredth Anniversary of the Printing of the English Bible," October 6, 1935, The American Presidency Project, UC Santa Barbara, https://www.presidency.ucsb.edu/documents/statement-the-four-hundredth-anniversary-the-printing-the-english-bible.
28. Calvin Coolidge to Eugene E. Thompson, Washington, March 31, 1927, in "Coolidge Declares Bible a Bulwark," *New York Times*, April 4, 1927, https://timesmachine.nytimes.com/timesmachine/1927/04/04/118641381.html.
29. "Nation Greets Mission Societies," *New York Times*, April 22, 1900, https://timesmachine.nytimes.com/timesmachine/1900/04/22/issue.html.
30. Ronald Reagan, "Remarks at the Annual Convention of the National Religious Broadcasters," January 31, 1983, Ronald Reagan Presidential Library & Museum, National Archives, https://www.reaganlibrary.gov/archives/speech/remarks-annual-convention-national-religious-broadcasters-0.
31. Harry S. Truman, "Address Before the Attorney General's Conference on Law Enforcement Problems," February 15, 1950, The American Presidency Project, UC Santa Barbara, https://www.presidency.ucsb.edu/documents/address-before-the-attorney-generals-conference-law-enforcement-problems.
32. "Scout Ban on Atheists Is Upheld," *Chicago Tribune*, May 18,

1993, https://www.chicagotribune.com/1993/05/18/scout-ban-on-atheists-is-upheld/.

33. Letter from John McLean, Chapel Wood, November 4, 1852, in *The National Magazine*, ed. Abel Stevens (Carlton & Phillips, 1854), 280.
34. John. F. Kennedy, "Inaugural Address, January 20, 1961," John F. Kennedy Presidential Library And Museum, https://www.jfklibrary.org/archives/other-resources/john-f-kennedy-speeches/inaugural-address-19610120.
35. Julia Ward Howe, "Battle Hymn of the Republic," February 1862, in "The Poems (We Think) We Know: 'Battle Hymn of the Republic,'" by Alexandra Socarides, *Los Angeles Review of Books*, November 11, 2013, https://lareviewofbooks.org/article/the-poems-we-think-we-know-battle-hymn-of-the-republic/.
36. Socarides, "The Poems (We Think) We Know."
37. "Government of Pocasset," March 7, 1638, Teaching American History, Ashbrook Center at Ashland University, https://teachingamericanhistory.org/document/government-of-pocasset/.
38. *Charter of Privileges Granted by William Penn, Esq. to the Inhabitants of Pennsylvania and Territories*, October 28, 1701, transcript, The Avalon Project, Yale Law School, https://avalon.law.yale.edu/18th_century/pa07.asp.
39. Joshua F. Speed, *Reminiscences of Abraham Lincoln* (Bradley & Gilbert, 1896), 32–33.
40. Eisenhower to the Advertising Men's Post of the American Legion, June 6, 1944, in "D-Day Gives Eisenhower 'Relaxation, Off Campus,' *New York Times*, June 7, 1949, https://timesmachine.nytimes.com/timesmachine/1949/06/07/84269893.html.
41. Eisenhower to the American Bible Society, in *Mason City Globe-Gazette*, November 16, 1956, Newspapers.com.
42. "Welcome to Levi and Catharine Coffin," Levi and Catharine Coffin State Historic Site, Indiana Museum and Historic Sites, accessed November 11, 2025, https://www.indianamuseum.org/historic-sites/levi-and-catharine-coffin-state-historic-site/.
43. Levi Coffin, *Reminiscences of Levi Coffin, The Reputed President of the Underground Railroad* (Robert Clarke, 1880), 578.

44. *Church of the Holy Trinity v. United States*, 143 U.S. 457, 471 (1892).
45. *Church of the Holy Trinity*, 143 U.S. at 466–470.
46. Jedidiah Morse, *A Sermon Exhibiting the Present Dangers, and Consequent Duties of the Citizens of the United States of America* (Samuel Etheridge, 1799), 10–11, Internet Archive.
47. "'I Wish There Were Words to Describe What It's Like,'" *Orlando Sentinel*, November 2, 1998, https://www.orlandosentinel.com/1998/11/02/i-wish-there-were-words-to-describe-what-its-like/.
48. Sarah J. Hale to Abraham Lincoln, Philadelphia, September 28, 1863, Abraham Lincoln Papers, Library of Congress, transcribed by Lincoln Studies Center, Knox College, https://www.loc.gov/static/classroom-materials/thanksgiving/documents/sarah_hale.pdf.
49. "Abraham Lincoln's Proclamation of Thanksgiving," October 3, 1863, American Battlefield Trust, https://www.battlefields.org/learn/primary-sources/abraham-lincolns-proclamation-thanksgiving.
50. Daniel Webster, *An Address Delivered Before the New York Historical Society* (Press of the Historical Society, 1852), 47.
51. Letter from Benjamin Silliman, New Haven, December 10, 1853, in *Testimony of Distinguished Laymen to the Value of the Sacred Scriptures, Particularly in Their Bearing on Civil and Social Life* (American Bible Society, 1854), 63.
52. "First Inaugural Address of Franklin D. Roosevelt," March 4, 1933, The Avalon Project, Yale Law School, https://avalon.law.yale.edu/20th_century/froos1.asp.
53. "Inaugural Address of Rutherford B. Hayes," March 5, 1877, The Avalon Project, Yale Law School, https://avalon.law.yale.edu/19th_century/hayes.asp.
54. "Ulysses S. Grant," April 27, 1922, Calvin Coolidge Presidential Foundation, https://coolidgefoundation.org/resources/ulysses-s-grant/. This was an address given by Vice President Calvin Coolidge at the dedication of the Ulysses S. Grant Memorial in Washington, D.C.
55. Maria Campbell, *Revolutionary Services and Civil Life of General William Hull* (D. Appleton, 1847), 38.

56. John Adams to Abigail Adams, April 26, 1777, Founders Online, National Archives, https://founders.archives.gov/documents/Adams/04-02-02-0169.
57. Fanny Crosby, "Blessed Assurance," 1873, Hymnary.org, https://hymnary.org/media/fetch/97642.
58. *Zorach v. Clauson*, 343 U.S. 306, 312–315 (1952).
59. James Madison, "Memorial and Remonstrance Against Religious Assessments [ca. 20 June 1785]," Founders Online, National Archives, https://founders.archives.gov/documents/Madison/01-08-02-0163.
60. "The Presbyterian Beginnings of Fundamentalism," Presbyterian Historical Society Blog, Presbyterian Church (U.S.A.), April 13, 2015, https://pcusa.org/news-storytelling/blogs/historical-society-blog/beginnings-fundamentalism.
61. "Patrick Henry—Give Me Liberty or Give Me Death," March 23, 1775, The Avalon Project, Yale Law School, https://avalon.law.yale.edu/18th_century/patrick.asp.
62. "Patrick Henry—Give Me Liberty or Give Me Death."
63. "Jarena Lee and the Early A.M.E. Church," National Museum of African American History and Culture, Smithsonian Institution, accessed December 15, 2025, https://nmaahc.si.edu/explore/stories/jarena-lee-and-early-ame-church.
64. Declaration of Independence, July 4, 1776, transcript, National Archives, https://www.archives.gov/founding-docs/declaration-transcript.
65. Coretta Scott King, "Remarks on the Introduction of the Employment Non-Discrimination Act of 1994—June 23, 1994," Archives of Women's Political Communication, Iowa State University, https://awpc.cattcenter.iastate.edu/2017/03/09/remarks-on-the-introduction-of-the-employment-non-discrimination-act-of-1994-june-23-1994/.
66. Abraham Lincoln, "Proclamation 97—Appointing a Day of National Humiliation, Fasting, and Prayer," March 30, 1863, The American Presidency Project, UC Santa Barbara, https://www.presidency.ucsb.edu/documents/proclamation-97-appointing-day-national-humiliation-fasting-and-prayer.
67. "About Us," Shields of Strength, accessed November 5, 2025,

https://www.shieldsofstrength.com/about-us/; Annie Gowen, "Father's Salute to a Son with 'a Big Heart': Army Ranger Is Arlington Cemetery's 1st Iraq Casualty," *Washington Post*, April 11, 2003, https://www.washingtonpost.com/archive/politics/2003/04/11/fathers-salute-to-a-son-with-a-big-heart/8b8db9b4-49f0-459a-a39f-4a1e7fe27081/; Matthew Cox, "Army Capt. Russell B. Rippetoe Died April 3, 2003 Serving During Operation Iraqi Freedom," Honor the Fallen, *Military Times*, accessed November 8, 2025, https://thefallen.militarytimes.com/army-capt-russell-b-rippetoe/256563.

68. *Marsh v. Chambers*, 463 U.S. 783, 790 (1983).
69. *Chambers v. Marsh*, 504 F. Supp. 585, 588 (D. Neb. 1980).
70. Benjamin Franklin Butler, "The Bible the Great Moral Renovator of Our Race," in *History of the American Bible Society from Its Organization to the Present Time* by W. P. Strickland (Harper & Brothers, 1850), 430.
71. Booker T. Washington, *Up from Slavery: An Autobiography* (1901, Project Gutenberg, 2025), chap. 7, https://www.gutenberg.org/ebooks/2376.
72. Laura Ross, "The Complete List of Kraft Heinz Brands," Thomas, August 5, 2024, https://www.thomasnet.com/insights/kraft-heinz-companies/.
73. Henry J. Heinz, will dated January 11, 1919, probated May 26, 1919, vol. 17, page 57, Register of Wills of Allegheny County, Pennsylvania, PA, 1, Detre Library and Archives, Senator John Heinz History Center.
74. John Hughes to the Stamp Act Commission, January 13, 1766, quoted in John C. Miller, *Origins of the American Revolution* (Stanford University Press, 1943), 196.
75. *The First Charter of Virginia*, April 10, 1606, transcript, The Avalon Project, Yale Law School, https://avalon.law.yale.edu/17th_century/va01.asp#1.
76. Mayflower Compact, 1620, transcript, The Avalon Project, Yale Law School, https://avalon.law.yale.edu/17th_century/mayflower.asp.
77. "Of Plimoth Plantation: Manuscript, 1630–1650," by William

Bradford, State Library of Massachusetts Digital Collections, http://archives.lib.state.ma.us/handle/2452/208249.

78. "History & Culture," Washington Monument, National Park Service, updated December 22, 2022, https://www.nps.gov/wamo/learn/historyculture/index.htm.
79. Morrow Coffey Graham, *They Call Me Mother Graham: The Power of Christ in a Home* (Billy Graham Evangelistic Association, 2007), 42.
80. *Vidal v. Girard's Executors*, 43 U.S. 127, 200 (1844).
81. *Vidal v. Girard's Executors*, 43 U.S. at 200.
82. Simon Greenleaf, *The Testimony of the Evangelists: Examined by the Rules of Evidence Administered in Courts of Justice* (James Cockcroft, 1874), vii–viii.
83. Charles Malik, "A Foreigner Looks at the United States," *Journal of General Education* 5, no. 4 (1951): 243, JSTOR.
84. Robert C. Winthrop, "The Bible: An Address Delivered at the Annual Meeting of the Massachusetts Bible Society in Boston, May 28, 1849," in *Addresses and Speeches on Various Occasions* (Little, Brown, 1852), 171–72.
85. Henry Augustus Muhlenberg, *The Life of Major-General Peter Muhlenberg* (Carey and Hart, 1849), 53.
86. "Patrick Henry—Give Me Liberty or Give Me Death," March 23, 1775, The Avalon Project, Yale Law School, https://avalon.law.yale.edu/18th_century/patrick.asp.
87. Declaration of Independence.
88. Declaration of Independence.
89. "Patrick Henry—Give Me Liberty or Give Me Death," March 23, 1775, The Avalon Project, Yale Law School, https://avalon.law.yale.edu/18th_century/patrick.asp.
90. James Patterson and Peter Kim, *The Day America Told the Truth: What People Really Believe About Everything That Really Matters* (Prentice Hall, 1991), 28.
91. Jonathan Edwards, *A Faithful Narrative of the Surprising Work of God, in the Conversion of Many Hundred Souls in Northampton* (1738), 39.
92. Katie Lange, "Pfc. Desmond Doss: The Unlikely Hero Behind 'Hacksaw Ridge,'" U.S. Army, February 28, 2017, https://www

.army.mil/article/183328/pfc_desmond_doss_the_unlikely_hero_behind_hacksaw_ridge; Tom Infield Knight-Ridder, "Okinawa Remembered Tales of Heroism, Horror Still Vivid for the Men Who Fought the Last Major Battle in the Pacific," *The Spokesman-Review*, April 2, 1995, https://www.spokesman.com/stories/1995/apr/02/okinawa-remembered-tales-of-heroism-horror-still/.

93. Kali Martin, "Private First Class Desmond Thomas Doss Medal of Honor," The National WWII Museum, October 12, 2020, https://www.nationalww2museum.org/war/articles/private-first-class-desmond-thomas-doss-medal-of-honor.
94. John C. Hamilton, *History of the Republic of the United States of America, as Traced in the Writings of Alexander Hamilton and of His Contemporaries*, vol. 7 (J. B. Lippincott, 1864), 790.
95. Charles F. Browne as Artemus Ward, "Fourth of July Oration," Weathersfield, Connecticut, July 4, 1859, in *The Complete Works of Artemus Ward* (G. W. Carleton, 1875), 118, revised for clarity.
96. Donald S. Lutz, "The Relative Influence of European Writers on Late Eighteenth-Century American Political Thought," *The American Political Science Review* 78, no. 1 (1984), https://doi.org/10.2307/1961257.
97. "Proclamation 4999—National Family Week, 1982," November 12, 1982, Ronald Reagan Presidential Library & Museum, National Archives, https://www.reaganlibrary.gov/archives/speech/proclamation-4999-national-family-week-1982.
98. Ezra Stiles, "The United States Elevated to Glory and Honor," 1783, ed. Reiner Smolinski, The University of Nebraska–Lincoln, 38–87, https://digitalcommons.unl.edu/cgi/viewcontent.cgi?article=1041&context=etas, spelling and capitalization revised for modernity.
99. General Douglas MacArthur, "Sylvanus Thayer Award Acceptance Address," speech, recorded May 12, 1962, American Rhetoric, audio and transcript, https://www.americanrhetoric.com/speeches/douglasmacarthurthayeraward.html.
100. David McCullough, *Truman* (Touchstone, 1992), 598.
101. "Recognition of Israel," Harry S. Truman Library & Museum, National Archives, accessed November 12, 2025, https://www.trumanlibrary.gov/museum/ordinary-man/recognition-of-israel.

102. Benjamin Franklin to Joseph Huey, Philadelphia, June 6, 1756, in *The Works of Benjamin Franklin*, vol. 3, ed. John Bigelow (G. P. Putnam's Sons, 1904), https://oll.libertyfund.org/titles/bigelow-the-works-of-benjamin-franklin-vol-iii-letters-and-misc-writings-1753-1763.
103. Ken Durham, "Robert Gilmour LeTourneau: Pioneer of Earth-Moving Equipment and Philanthropist," Texas State Historical Association, updated January 10, 2001, https://www.tshaonline.org/handbook/entries/letourneau-robert-gilmour.
104. R. G. LeTourneau, *Mover of Men and Mountains: The Autobiography of R. G. LeTourneau* (Moody, 1967), 110.
105. Samuel Colgate, in Stephen Abbott Northrop *A Cloud of Witnesses: The Greatest Men in the World for Christ and the Book* (Christian Evidence, 1902), 93.
106. *Resolution of the House of Burgesses Designating a Day of Fasting and Prayer*, May 24, 1774, transcript, Founders Online, National Archives, https://founders.archives.gov/documents/Jefferson/01-01-02-0082.
107. "Blackstone's Commentaries on the Laws of England," The Avalon Project, Yale Law School, 39–42, https://avalon.law.yale.edu/18th_century/blackstone_intro.asp#2.
108. "InFaith Heritage," InFaith, The American Missionary Fellowship, accessed November 13, 2025, https://infaith.org/about/heritage.
109. David Francis, *Missionary Sunday School* (LifeWay, 2011), 15.
110. B. Paxson Drury, *A Fruitful Life: A Narrative of the Adventures and Missionary Labors of Stephen Paxson* (Rice & Hirst, 1882), 22, 185.
111. Patrick Henry, in William Wirt, *Sketches of the Life and Character of Patrick Henry* (James Webster, 1817), 58.
112. Calvin Coolidge, "The Destiny of America," Northampton, Memorial Day, 1923, Calvin Coolidge Presidential Foundation, https://coolidgefoundation.org/resources/vice-president-1921-1923-13/.
113. "Asbury, Francis—Timeline Biography," The Association of Religion Data Archives, accessed November 13, 2025, https://www.thearda.com/us-religion/history/timelines/entry?etype=5&eid=79.

114. Nathan O. Hatch, "The Puzzle of American Methodism," *Church History* 63, no. 2 (1994), 178, https://doi.org/10.2307/3168586.
115. William Samuel Johnson, E. Edwards Beardsley, in *Life and Times of William Samuel Johnson, LL. D.* (Hurd and Houghton, 1876), 141–42.
116. Evan Thomas, "An American Hero," *Newsweek*, June 18, 1995, https://www.newsweek.com/american-hero-183766.
117. William D. Montalbano, "It's the 4th of July in June for Pilot," *Los Angeles Times*, June 10, 1995, https://www.latimes.com/archives/la-xpm-1995-06-10-mn-11703-story.html.
118. *Britannica*, "The New England Colonies," updated November 14, 2025, https://www.britannica.com/place/United-States/The-New-England-colonies.
119. John Winthrop, "A Model of Christian Charity," December 31, 1630, ed. Sarah Morgan Smith et al., Teaching American History, https://teachingamericanhistory.org/document/a-model-of-christian-charity-2/.
120. *Winthrop's Journal*, vol. 2, *1630–1649*, Original Narratives of Early American History, ed. J. Franklin Jameson (Charles Scribner's Sons, 1908), 100.
121. *The Fundamental Orders of Connecticut*, January 14, 1639, transcript, ed. Gordon Lloyd, Teaching American History, https://teachingamericanhistory.org/document/the-fundamental-orders-of-connecticut/.
122. Franklin D. Roosevelt, "Prayer on D-Day," June 6, 1944, The American Presidency Project, UC Santa Barbara, https://www.presidency.ucsb.edu/documents/prayer-d-day.
123. "America on Its Knees Poster," 1952, The Lincoln Financial Foundation Collection, Indiana State Museum, https://www.lincolncollection.org/collection/categories/item/?cat=14&page=14&pagesize=36&view=gallery&item=102425.

# About the Authors

**Dr. Richard Lee** is founding pastor of First Redeemer Church, Atlanta, and speaker for the award-winning *There's Hope America* television series. He is widely recognized as a popular spokesman on the influence of America's religious history and its impact on today's culture. Dr. Lee is a frequent speaker at national conventions and on university campuses and media outlets across the country, including FOX News, Fox Business News, CBS News, the BBC, and CNN. His articles have appeared in publications such as *USA Today*, *London Times*, *L.A. Times*, *Essence*, and *Newsweek*. He is the author of eighteen books, including *The American Patriots Bible*, which reached the number five spot on Amazon.com's bestseller list. Dr. Lee was educated at Mercer University and Luther Rice Seminary with postdoctoral studies at Oxford University. He also serves as a member of the prestigious Oxford Round Table, Oxford, England.

**Jack Countryman** is the founder of JCountryman gift books, a division of Thomas Nelson, and is the recipient of the Evangelical Christian Publishers Association's Kip Jordan Lifetime Achievement Award. Over the past 30 years, he has developed bestselling gift books such as *God's Promises for Your Every Need*, *God's Promises for Men*, *God's Promises for Women*, *God Listens*, and *Red Letter Words of Jesus*. Countryman's books have sold more than 27 million copies. His graduation books alone have sold nearly 2 million copies.